THE SOUL OF
THE LAW

THE SOUL OF
THE LAW

BENJAMIN SELLS

ELEMENT

Rockport, Massachussetts • Shaftesbury, Dorset
Brisbane, Queensland

Soul of the Law

Published in the USA in 1994 by
Element Books, Inc.
PO Box 830, Rockport, MA 01966

Published in Great Britain in 1994 by
Element Books Limited
Shaftesbury, Dorset SP7 8BP

Published in Australia in 1994 by
Element Books Limited for
Jacaranda Wiley Limited
33 Park Road, Milton, Brisbane 4064

First paperback edition 1996

Cover and text design by Paperwork, Ithica, New York

Typeset by Moonlight Graphics

Printed and bound in the United States of America by
Edwards Brothers, Inc.
Library of Congress Cataloging in Publication data available
British Library Cataloguing in Publication data available

ISBN 1–85230–796–X

Author and publisher gratefully acknowledge the permission to quote
portions of the following copyright sources: *InterViews*, Spring
Publications, Dallas, 1983 by James Hillman with Laura Pozzo;
"Lawyers in Distress" by A. Elwork and G. Benjamin, 1993; "The Effect
of Legal Education on Attitudes," L. Eron and R. Redmount, *Journal of
Legal Education* 1957 (copyright is held by the Association of American
Law Schools).

CONTENTS

To Rima

FOREWORD

WE ARE LIVING in a time when soul is being drained from the very social institutions that are supposed to be preserving life and values. We see signs of this drain in language that has become manipulative and empty, in the anemic condition of ethics and morality, and in the hunger for real pleasure and meaningful lives that even affluent and successful people confess to.

Feeling our own weakening of courage and vitality we are tempted to ask the wrong questions: Why is this happening now? What are we doing wrong? What historical or evolutionary development is the cause of our trouble? These questions don't go deep enough. They are narcissistic, assuming that we are the center of this universe in entropy.

But soul cannot be regained through clever insights and muscled projects of improvement. It returns only when deep vision has been restored, when imagination revivifies, and when we allow ourselves to feel the soul's complaints so that we can find our way back to necessary sensitivities.

This exceptional book avoids the tempting but wrong questions, and inquires sensitively into the current weakened condition of the soul of the law. The author brings expertise and experience from three areas—law, psychotherapy, and philosophy—to bear on the issues he raises, and he uses language that has body and context. In other words, he conjures up soul in his own writing as a means of initiating the process of finding law's soul.

Each reader should take this book up as a guide for meditation on the reader's own situation, and not as a solution to some abstract problem with law. Excessive abstraction and problem-solving are signs of the very modernity that Benjamin Sells says is at the root of the law's suffering soul. If the law were to regain its soul, we would all, not only lawyers, benefit from the conviviality that law, at its best, can offer people in need of the pleasure of one another's company.

THOMAS MOORE
Author, *Care of the Soul*

ACKNOWLEDGEMENTS

ALTHOUGH THIS BOOK bears my name alone, it is not the result of a solitary effort. It contains ideas and insights given generously by many people who must unfortunately go unnamed. But a few people were so instrumental to this work, so essential to it, that their names belong here:

To Rima Čepėnas, my wife, for the inspiring beauty of her soul, and in whose love and confidence all things seem possible;

To Thomas Moore, my friend, teacher, and colleague, for his abiding affection, patient wisdom, and steadfast encouragement over many years;

To James Hillman for his courage and voice;

To Paul Cash, my editor at Element Books, for his care and attention to both the big ideas and the small necessities, and for his gentle proddings;

To Bruce Rubenstein and Chuck Carmen of *Illinois Legal Times*, for giving me a place to start; and

To the many lawyers who daily do the difficult work of peacemaking, and for whom this book was written,

Thank you.

INTRODUCTION

ONCE, when I was still practicing law, my wife's car started acting up so she took it to the garage. That evening I asked her what the mechanic had said, and she told me, thinking that was the end of it. But then I started:

"Did you ask him about the rattle?"

"No, I didn't."

"When he said it was the fuel injector, did you ask him whether it was a common problem or if maybe there was something more serious? Maybe a design flaw or something?"

"No," she said, looking at me a little strangely.

"Did you ask him . . ."

"You're cross-examining me!" she said finally, to which I responded as would any lawyer accused of such a thing:

"I am not!"

Now I know my wife knows just as much about cars as I do, and is certainly more than able to handle a trip to a garage without my help. So this wasn't some kind of I'm-the-man-and-know-all-about-cars thing. No, something else had happened, something having to do with my being a lawyer. Because she was right—I was cross-examining her. It wasn't even the content of my questions so much as the *persistent style* of my inquiries, as if I were trying to cover every base, probe every possibility, close every door.

The more I thought about it, the more I came to realize two crucial things about that exchange. First, I hadn't intended to cross-examine my wife. Second, I hadn't been aware that I was doing so. What was going on?

I began to watch and listen to myself and my lawyer friends when we were in non-legal settings. I found that, like me, they too sounded like lawyers almost all the time. Their style of speaking, choice of words, even their physical posturing and bodily gestures had a kind of studied and measured quality that seemed to me to be continuations of their professional demeanor. In those few instances where I knew folks well enough to risk starting a fight, I would ask their friends, lovers, and family if they noticed these lawyerly mannerisms. Repeatedly, these people would instantly nod their heads and say they knew *exactly* what I was talking about while the lawyers, just as I had done with my wife, would deny that they were "acting like lawyers."

This situation was especially interesting to me given my background as a psychotherapist. Before becoming a lawyer, I had done my graduate work in philosophical psychology and religious studies, and in particular was drawn to the work of depth psychologists such as Freud and Jung, and that of James Hillman, Thomas Moore, and others working under the general mantle of archetypal or imaginal psychology. Throughout their work, I found, in varying forms, the recurring idea of enduring psychological patterns working in and through the soul. Many archetypal and imaginal psychologists tend to focus on images drawn from mythology as examples of these enduring patterns; they talk about things like the Hero, Great Mother, Trickster, and so on. For my part, however, I have always been more interested in the soul's less grandiose, more mundane styles of self-expression. For example, say we both know a person and I am telling you a story about something that person said. You listen to the story and then say "You know, that's just like her," or "I can just hear her saying that." What you are pointing to is a kind of cohesion, a natural proclivity, a certain style that she embodies. People's personalities seem to hold together in identifiable ways, and it might even be fair to say that a person's individuality comes from this blending of the unique and the predictable.

The more I thought about it, the clearer it became that my unconscious cross-examining of my wife was more than just a personal quirk. All around me I saw and heard other lawyers doing the same thing. It didn't take long before I became convinced that professions, like people, can be seen as having their own personalities and that these professional personalities, too, are blendings of the unique and the predictable. Furthermore, it became apparent to me that these professional personalities exert considerable influence on the lives of the people in the profession. Cross-examining my wife might have been out of character for me, for example, but it wasn't out of character for the legal profession.

Like people, professions have certain ways of looking at things, harbor their own peculiar prejudices, and exhibit their own particular styles. This is probably true of all human endeavors, but I don't recall having seen it with such clarity outside of the so-called professions. I mean, I was a bartender, too, but nobody ever told me I was talking to them like a bartender. It's as if professions exert a deeper influence on the lives of their practitioners than do mere occupations or jobs. After all, in our society a person is said to "become" a lawyer or a doctor or an architect, suggesting a melding of identities between the practitioner and the profession.

Like people, professions are more than the sum of their parts. Like people, professions are driven and sustained by invisible desires. And, like people, professions like to proclaim their own uniqueness and will go to great pains to show how they are different from other professions. Professions want to be respected for what they are. They want to be understood, appreciated, even loved.

The individual practitioner is charged with the responsibility of living up to these larger, enduring professional desires. One might even say that professions live vicariously through the lives of their practitioners, that the practitioner always lives at least two lives—the usual life of the lay person and the larger-than-human life of the profession. Not surprisingly, this dual existence can raise questions as to how to distinguish between the two. The practitioner must always ask Who am I doing this act for? Who is thinking this thought? To be a professional is to be inhabited, sometimes possessed, by another voice.

Lawyers form an identifiable group. This is not to say that there aren't differences among individual lawyers, but the very fact that lawyers are identifiable as a group suggests the presence of unifying themes. These themes comprise the Law's self-image and are the psychological sources for the common attitudes that guide lawyers in their daily practice. What's more, these themes also influence how everyone who isn't a lawyer thinks, feels, and imagines about Law and lawyers in our world.

It is to this profound muddle that this book is dedicated. I want to explore the mysterious recurring themes that dominate the Law's psychological existence and ask how these themes play out in the lives of lawyers and others who find themselves for one reason or another involved either with the Law or with a lawyer, which in this day and age probably means just about everyone. To do this means always starting from two places at once: with lawyers as the clearest living embodiments of the Law in our culture; and with the powerful, almost divine influences of the Law as a psychological reality in its own right. On the one hand, what does the Law want? What are its hidden desires? How does it think? How does it imagine? What does it dream? On the other hand, how do the Law's expectations and attitudes affect the lawyer's personal and private life? What does it mean to "become a lawyer," to "think like a lawyer"? Are there points of conflict between the lawyer's personal values and those of the legal profession? What does the lawyer get in return for his or her dedicated service to the Law? And most important, if I am to be true to my own profession's namesake ("psychotherapy" literally means "care of the soul"), what does all of this portend for the soul?

III

These are not idle inquiries. The Law is said to be one of the pillars of civilization, one of humankind's great achievements. Some even say Law separates human from beast. In the political arena, our ideas and attitudes about the Law shape how we think about our society, how it should be governed and what are the natural limits of that governance. How we think about the Law determines in large part how we settle our differences, just as we also rely on the Law to protect our right to *be* different. History tells us that our country is a country of laws, and that no person is above the Law. In short, it has gotten to the point that it is almost impossible for us to imagine life without Law.

And yet the soul of the Law is suffering.

Everywhere you look nowadays, the symptoms of this suffering are apparent. In the courts, where the Law seems most at home, litigants are unable to have their cases heard because of an onslaught of litigation unparalleled at any other time or in any other place. Some politicians warn that we are suing ourselves into economic stagnation, while others rabidly defend the "right" to sue over the least little thing. Across the nation, judges retire in disgust and helplessness after years on the bench, their twelve-hour days unable to dent an ever-mounting backlog of cases. Lawyers are forced to tell clients that although they are indeed entitled to their day in court they might not live long enough to see it.

The legal profession itself shows similar symptoms of distress. Incivility among lawyers has increased to the point where some courts are calling for the adoption of codes of conduct for lawyers in an attempt to de-escalate winner-take-all battles that undermine centuries of collegiality and mutual respect. Firms of long standing are collapsing as lawyers decide to go it on their own in a desperate attempt to make more money, often leaving in disarray or ruin the places that made their individual success possible in the first place. Loyalty, even among lawyers in the same firm, has disintegrated to the point where many lawyers say it no longer exists. The movement of partners among law firms, a relative rarity only a few years ago, is now commonplace, and nowadays it is the rare associate who retires from the same firm at which he or she started their career.

And then there is the individual lawyer. Report after report tells us that lawyers experience psychological unrest at much higher levels than non-lawyers. A survey of 105 occupations showed lawyers first on the list in experiencing depression; another study reports that fully *one third* of all attorneys suffer from either depression, alcohol or drug abuse (substance abuse is so bad that some attorney disciplinary groups estimate upwards of seventy-five percent of all complaints against lawyers involve substance abuse); anxiety and obsessive behavior afflict a disproportionately large number of lawyers, sometimes to the point of incapacitation; many lawyers report strong feelings of isolation and social alienation; and upwards of sixty percent of lawyers say they would not recommend the law as a career to their own children. Worst of all, the most common psychological complaints by lawyers are feelings of inadequacy and inferiority in relationships. Lawyers in today's world are lonely, painfully lonely.

Prevailing wisdom says that such problems are caused by

stress, which in turn is caused primarily by increased economic and competitive pressures accompanying a shift from law as a profession to law as a business. But such an analysis falls pitifully short, and, as we shall see, is in fact symptomatic of the very things that ail the legal soul.

We shall take a different tack, asking not so much about what managerial or organizational changes need to be made to "fix" things, although there certainly is room for innovation here, but instead lending a willing and sympathetic ear to the Law's own voice. What is the soul of the Law trying to tell us through its symptoms? I take it as something of a psychological maxim that symptoms always perform at least a dual role, pointing in very particular terms to the place that hurts while at the same time suggesting how we might respond to the pain. If the history of psychology teaches us anything, it is that the soul reveals itself most vividly in its unrest; and so we shall take time to listen to the Law's symptoms just as they appear without attempting in the first instance to eradicate them. We must remember that our concern is for the soul of the Law and see the Law's symptoms as opportunities for soulful insight.

A reporter once asked me whether feelings like depression and alienation are part of the legal profession itself or of individual lawyers. Another acquaintance asked if such symptoms appear in the legal profession because the people who become lawyers are already predisposed to such psychological complaints. These curious questions point to the mysterious relationship between Law and Lawyer. Both questions rest on a particularly American viewpoint that grants priority to the individual and claims that communities are merely groups of individual volunteers. According to this view, problems appearing within a community can be traced to the individuals who make up the community, and to improve the community we must therefore begin with the individual. This viewpoint, fueled now by centuries of political and psychological theory, claims that if we fix the individual the rest will follow.

There are many problems with this kind of excessive individualism. For our purposes, one of the most important is that it deprives communities of their own individuality and integrity while also depriving the individual of a sense of intrinsic community. As with all dualisms, the problem with the individual/ community dichotomy lies in the "/."

Most lawyers, if pressed, will acknowledge a feeling that somehow they are part of something bigger than themselves, something that cannot be reduced to a mere collection of individuals, something distinguishable from them as individuals. *It is this sense that I want to entertain and encourage.* If, as we shall see, many of the psychological problems facing the Law and lawyers result from excessive individualism, then perhaps we can respond to these symptoms in part by re-visioning how we think about individuality.

To care for the soul of the Law we must enter into and sustain this mystery and *resist falling into self-help simplicity.* One way to avoid this modern trap is to return to older, more respectful ways of imagining the relationship between the human and the larger world. A particularly appealing image, and one I adopt as the structure for this work, is that of macrocosm, or great world, and microcosm, or little world. According to this view— especially as formulated in the work of Neoplatonic thinkers such as Plotinus, Marsilio Ficino, and Paracelsus—the human as microcosm is like the greater world in miniature, a kind of embodied reflection, and the two are intimately connected through a deep sympathy. What happens in the greater world happens in the little world, and vice versa. One of the beautiful things about this image is how it blurs modern dichotomies like individual and community, human and world, I and Thou. Human as microcosm cannot be reduced to a isolated entity acting mechanically within a larger, detached environment. Instead, the human is held to be part of the environment, a mirror reflecting environmental concerns while also casting its own reflection into a receptive world. Applied to the legal profession, this view enables us to re-think the relationship between Law and lawyer. No longer can the legal profession be reduced to a collection of discrete and ultimately isolated individuals; no longer can lawyers be seen as islands.

As we shall see over and over again, there are intimate and indissoluble links between the broader breakdowns evident in the legal profession and the psychological complaints of individual lawyers. Each carries the imagination of the other, influences the other. Soul-work requires us to immerse ourselves in this eternal tension between macrocosm and microcosm, seeking not only intellectual understanding but a more aesthetic, perhaps even erotic, appreciation born of the heart. Because one can never place responsibility for a suffering soul with any degree of certainty, we will not indulge in useless finger-pointing or the gamesmanship of blame. Instead we will try simply to attend the creative tension that constitutes both Law and lawyer. Perhaps the first step in caring for a troubled soul is to realize that we cannot have one in the absence of the other.

MACROCOSM
LAW AND PROFESSION

CHAPTER ONE
WHAT DOES THE LAW WANT?

THE MOST important first step in understanding anything psychologically is to get an image. Images are more complete, more fertile, than concepts because they have a broader range of expression and are therefore more precise. Also, images allow our personal perspectives to coalesce with more enduring psychic patterns. So, in turning a psychological eye to the Law, we first need an *image* of what we are talking about.

I ask the reader to conduct the following experiment:

Imagine you are a psychotherapist. It's mid-afternoon on a Wednesday in October. You're sitting in your office, catching up on some mail. Your next session isn't for a couple of hours, and you're just getting ready to start a letter to a colleague when a knock comes on your door. You quickly double-check your appointment book to make sure you haven't forgotten someone, but no, the blank lines confirm that no one is due until four. You open the door and a person is standing there whom you have never seen before, but who bears a certain distant familiarity.

"Hello," says the person, "I'm the Law. I want to talk with you about some things."

"Come in, come in," you say, not really sure what to make out of this.

"I'm sorry to show up without an appointment," says the Law. "But I just happened to be walking down the street and saw your sign out front. I hadn't really thought about coming to a therapist until about five minutes ago, but then I decided what the hell, I might as well give it a shot. Do you have some time to talk?"

"Sure," you say. "My next appointment isn't for a while yet. Here, let me take your coat. Would you like some coffee? Tea?"

Question One: **What does the person who has just walked into your office look like?** Be very precise, and try to imagine this person in detail. Is the Law male or female? Old, young, middle-aged? How is the Law dressed? What kind of coat did you take from the Law? Is the Law carrying anything? Does the Law prefer coffee or tea? How does the Law speak, move, sit? Can you see the Law's eyes? What are they like? Try to imagine the Law as clearly as you can, getting as full-fledged an image as possible. Concentrate on the details, and be as accurate as you can.

"So," you say as you both sit down, "what brings you here?"

"Like I said, I was just walking down the street and saw your sign."

"Was there anything in particular you wanted to talk about?"

The Law sits silently for a moment, and appears to be staring at something on the floor halfway between the two of you. Then the Law looks up and says "Yes, I guess there is something bothering me."

Question Two: **What does the Law say? What's bothering the Law?**

III

When I have done this experiment with groups, most people, men and women alike, say the Law is an older man, gray-haired and distinguished looking. There is some disagreement about how the Law is dressed, but most people say the coat is an expensive one, maybe camel or leather. Often the Law is carrying a briefcase, sometimes a newspaper or some books. And almost everyone says the Law is a coffee drinker, usually black with no sugar. On rare occasions, lawyers will say the Law is female. On rarer occasions someone will say the Law is both male and female. Other recurring details I've heard about this imaginary person are that the Law is brisk of movement, as if it has somewhere important to go, and that the Law speaks with a measured and careful voice. A few people have commented on the Law's eyes, some saying the Law has steady, piercing eyes while others see them as tired and bedraggled, the eyes of a person who has seen too much.

What did the Law say to you about its troubles? Again, I have found strong similarities in people's responses to this question. Often the Law says it is misunderstood and overworked. But when pressed about deeper concerns, people often imagine the Law saying it is "troubled," sometimes going so far as to use words such as alienated, isolated, anxious, depressed, besieged, and lonely.

Some people, especially lawyers, balk at such questions, finding them offensive or perhaps suspecting they conceal a hidden agenda of some sort. These folks usually maintain that the entire exercise is silly, arguing that you can't personalize an abstraction so it makes no sense to ask whether the Law is male or female, and that this kind of imaginary, fictional exercise is too "touchy-feely" to be of import. This resistance and antagonism to imagination is telling, and we will find it is a recurring theme in our work with the Law.

III

"What do you mean when you say you're misunderstood?" you ask.

The Law leans back and brushes away an invisible speck of lint. "Well, people don't understand what I'm trying to do for them."

"Do you mean they don't understand intellectually, or they don't appreciate you?"

The Law begins to object to this little hop of interpretation, but then shrugs and says, "Both. They don't understand how I work, or how hard, and they don't appreciate how important I am. Perhaps that sounds arrogant to you, but the fact of the matter is that I don't know what might happen to the world without me."

"Let's come back to that later," you say, sensing that things are moving too fast, that important details are being skimmed over. You refill the Law's coffee and ask, "What is it you *want* exactly? I mean, if you could make things any way you want them to be so you wouldn't feel this way, what would you do?"

Question Three: What does the Law want? How would the Law change things?

"You said a minute ago that people don't realize how important you are. What makes you think that?"

"Are you kidding? My God, everyone bitches about me all

the time. I mean I'm O.K. as long as I apply to someone else, but as soon as I prohibit somebody's own pet behavior they go crazy. It's like I'm only supposed to apply to the other guy. And just look at how people talk about my representatives . . ."

"Representatives?" you ask.

"Lawyers," explains the Law. "All of this lawyer-bashing tries to make everything the lawyers' fault. That's just a roundabout way of attacking me, you know."

"But don't lots of people talk about how important the Law is?"

"Yes, almost always as a reaction to violence of some kind — you know, the Law and Order thing. People expect me to crack down on the bad guys but hate me when I try to keep *them* in line. Sometimes I feel like a toxic waste dump—not in my backyard."

"What if people did realize how important you are? How would they act differently from how they act now?"

"I don't want much. If people would just listen to what I tell them and obey me, show a little respect, that would be enough."

"You want to be obeyed?"

"Of course I do. That's what the Law is for isn't it?"

***Question Four:* Is that what the Law is for?**

"You say you want people to obey you, but they don't. Where does that leave you?"

"There's only one thing to do when people get unruly, and that's to force them to comply. Society can't exist without Law; people have to be made to respect and obey me."

"But isn't it impossible to force someone to respect something? I mean, maybe you can make them comply through force, but you can't instill respect that way."

The Law flushes a bit at this remark, and for a second seems on the verge of getting up to leave. You make a mental note that the Law doesn't like being contradicted. But then the Law composes itself, laces its fingers together in its lap and says with studied, almost condescending calm, "People respect strength. I know people don't like to be forced to do something, but it's for their own good. Over time, they'll see I am right."

"What do you think would happen to society without you?"

"Anarchy, pure and simple. Society needs me."

"And why exactly does your absence lead to anarchy?"

"Look at history!" The Law leans forward, hands open now. A point is about to be made. "Human nature has to be restrained. Without an orderly way of organizing society, of resolving disputes, and of ensuring that people do the right thing, we would have people killing each other over the slightest disagreement. Without me, people would shirk their responsibilities. They'd start making up their own ways of dealing with disputes. A lawless society cannot endure."

"But some people say that's pretty much how things are now, even with all the laws already on the book."

"That's just my point. The laws are there but people aren't obeying them. People are ignoring me, they're lawless."

"So what do you want to do about it?"

"There's only one thing you can do when people disobey the Law. You must enforce the Law—make them obey. Lock them up if necessary, fine them, take their rights away, whatever it takes. But the only way to establish and maintain order is through the Law."

III

We leave our imaginary therapy session now, but I encourage the reader (especially lawyers and law students) to pursue it further. This kind of active imagination is instructive on many levels, revealing not only our personal beliefs about the Law but also deeper, transpersonal themes that give insight into the Law's own personality. Just as novelists talk of their characters taking on a life of their own, so too the Law can be imagined as if it has a life of its own. *The Law that lives in our imagination is far more influential than we might think.* Usually it operates unconsciously, affecting our ideology, our everyday practice, how we think about the Law's role in society, how we relate to concepts like order and obedience, and how we understand larger themes like truth and justice.

The Law that lives in imagination can also offer insight into the Law's unrest. Already, in the short dialogue we have had with the Law, we get a feeling that the Law is bothered by something other than what it actually says, something only hinted at. As in any therapy, what the Law presents as the source of its discontent—people not understanding and not respecting it—is just a starting point for more subtle investigations.

ORDER, OBEDIENCE, OBSESSION

I have noticed an interesting difference in the responses of non-lawyers and lawyers regarding what the Law wants. Most non-lawyers say right off the bat that the Law wants justice. Lawyers, on the other hand, tend to be more diverse in their answers, mentioning things like equality, individual rights, truth, and fairness. It is not uncommon, for example, to hear lawyers say that what is legal doesn't necessarily have anything to do with what is just, or that truth and fairness are only ideals while the Law deals with practical reality. A surprising number of lawyers say none of these high-sounding ideals hit on what the Law wants, and that maintaining social order is the Law's prime concern. But one thing that does emerge when lawyers talk about these fundamental ideas is a kind of tentativeness, as if they aren't used to talking about such things and may even be a bit suspicious of big talk about justice and what have you. In the end, an uneasy consensus often emerges that holds justice up as an unattainable goal while emphasizing social order as an acceptable and achievable substitute.

Once the step is made from idealistic talk about justice to more pragmatic-sounding talk about social order, lawyers seem to be more comfortable. Not that there is agreement on how to achieve order, because there isn't. No, the comfort comes from the very *manner* of the talk, the structures and forms agreed to as the parameters of discussion. It's like scientists who disagree over a theory but nonetheless *do* agree on the efficacy of scientific proof, the use of mathematical forms, and the like. Once lawyers can translate a discussion into a give-and-take over rights and responsibilities they have shifted the discussion to their turf, and with this shift comes the comfort of familiarity. Lawyers, for example, might disagree over how to achieve the Law's desire for order while agreeing on things like the need for objective and dispassionate decision-making and the importance of set rules and regulations for ensuring due process, predictability of outcome, and uniformity of result.

I should add that not once, among all of the people I have talked to about the question of what the Law wants, has anyone ever said that the Law wants "peace." This is a significant point, I think, because it suggests that although the Law is interested in maintaining social order, it sees peace-making as something ultimately beyond its purview. At best, the Law seems to imagine itself as having a peace-keeping mission similar to that of a United Nations force that defines peace only as the absence of conflict. From this perspective, the Law is seen as an outside, occupying force responsible for imposing and maintaining order. As for encouraging a deeper sense of tolerance and understanding that might lead to a lasting peace, that is not the Law's job. The point here is not whether the Law should or should not think this way, but that it *does* tend to think this way and that this self-image has psychological implications.

One of these implications shows up in the Law's stated desire for order and obedience. What is curious here is the tension between the Law's desire to be understood and its more patronizing expectation to be obeyed. It's as if the Law confuses obedience with allegiance, forced acquiescence with willing acceptance. The Law even goes so far as to identify itself with obedience, saying obedience is "what the Law is for."

From a psychological perspective, the Law's identification with obedience and its single-minded emphasis on order have an obsessive ring. Obsession can be defined as a situation in which a single idea or image holds the mind captive, seeking to draw all other perspectives into itself. Usually obsession shows up in symptoms as a peculiar one-sidedness, as when the Law insists that it is misunderstood because others have failed in their obligation to understand it, and that without Law anarchy would necessarily follow. These obsessive ideas repress other possibilities. Perhaps the Law *itself* has failed to find ways to be understood communally, or perhaps the Law's desire for order and obedience is skewing its own self-understanding. Who knows, perhaps it is the Law and not others that needs to deepen its understanding. Perhaps it is the Law that lacks respect for people's natural resistance to its own obsessive desire for obedience and order. Such possibilities fall by the wayside because they are not allowed by the narrow constraints of the obsession.

The Law's obsession with order and obedience also manifests in practicalities: an ever increasing proliferation of legislation, rules, and regulations that suggest there must be a law for every problem; mandatory sentencing statutes decreeing that flexibility means weakness; strict rules of procedure and evidence that attempt to control every phase and detail of the legal process; excessive bureaucracy; courtroom architecture dominated by straight lines and authoritative decor including rows of benches, rectangular tables, elevated benches, fenced-off jury boxes and partitioned witness chairs; the tools of the legal trade with its uniform volumes of carefully indexed and cross-referenced books, and legal pads with their ruled lines; and even the very uniformity of dress and personal mannerism that so readily identifies a person as a lawyer—these things and many others like them suggest a constriction of imagination in favor of the controlling metaphors of order and obedience. "Law" and "Order" are so linked in our common imaginations that they seem to follow as one breath follows another.

Whenever people say they stand for or believe in a particular thing, they also are saying that they don't stand for or believe in a host of other things. That's what definition does. It marks boundaries and seeks to establish the identity of one thing through the exclusion of other things. If I say I'm a Democrat then I imply I'm not a Republican, if a Catholic then not a Protestant, etc. But exclusion by definition doesn't mean these other things necessarily disappear or don't continue to live within a person. I can be a Democrat in name and a Republican by temperament, or I can profess to be a Democrat but consistently vote Republican in the privacy of the voting booth.

The things we exclude through self-definition often reappear in subtle but extraordinarily powerful ways in our lives. Often there is friction between how we perceive ourselves and how others perceive us. Just think about the people you have known who claim to be one way, perhaps are even adamant about it, while their everyday actions reveal otherwise. In fact, one of the great things about being in close relationships is the chance to have running encounters with other people's perceptions of us, people who can be mirrors for our self-conceptions and help us to expand how we see and understand our own identities. But the chance to learn about ourselves from the perceptions of others breaks down if we define ourselves in an unduly narrow and restrictive fashion. Then we start to see symptoms associated with a closed-shop mentality—intolerance, suspicion of others, fear that if I am not the way I think I am then I'm nothing, and a kind of grandiosity masquerading as confidence. The more narrowly people define themselves, the more gets left out. And the more insistent a person is in denying these other possibilities, the more these possibilities live the life of the excluded—

constantly trying to find ways to break back into the person's life and gain respect, if not acceptance.

Clues about what is being excluded sometime come in the form of the moralisms we embrace without really thinking about them. The idea here is that we are most unconscious in those places we feel the most normal, mundane, and common-place—our unconsciousness of them is what makes them feel so normal. So when the Law easily identifies itself with order and obedience it is the very ease of this identification that draws our psychological interest. What exactly is the Law saying? What does it mean by order and obedience? Is it implying that disorder and disobedience are necessarily wrong? What is getting left out? Quite apart from whether such views are right or wrong, moral judgments are not without their psychological implications. Our psychological tradition teaches that the things we repress will eventually return in altered form—repressed sexuality returning as prudishness or in secret perversities, and so on. Furthermore, there seems to be a direct relationship between the force with which we repress things and the power with which they return. If so, then we might expect disorder and disobedience to reappear under various guises in the everyday life of the Law, especially in those places where the Law is most adamant in its demands for order and obedience.

DISORDERLY CONDUCT AND CIVIL DISOBEDIENCE

Despite the Law's concerns that lawlessness is breaking out in society, there is more than ample evidence that lawlessness is breaking out within the Law itself. For example, in the last several years there has been a disturbing rise in incivility among lawyers. Depending on which survey you choose, roughly half of all lawyers think there is a problem with incivility in the legal profession. One survey found that fifty-six percent of lawyers cite "obnoxiousness" as the most prevalent unpleasant quality they encounter in working with other lawyers. Mind you, this is what lawyers are saying about *themselves*.

There are many examples and many degrees of this new incivility: not returning phone calls, saying one thing to opposing counsel in the hall and another thing in front of the court, filing purposefully burdensome and far-reaching discovery requests in an effort to deplete and demoralize the other side, verbally abusing other lawyers and the court, lying, even physical violence. It seems to me that such conduct is a manifestation of precisely the kind of lawlessness that the Law is so concerned about. Why are the Law's own emissaries acting this way?

The usual answers given to this question have a kind of Pavlovian ring to them, positing external factors as stimuli that lawyers respond to with uncivilized conduct. The favorite explanation is that the practice of law is no longer a profession but a business in which concerns for the "bottom line" have supplanted concerns for civility. Stimulus: economic pressure. Response: incivility as lawyers compete for pieces of a smaller pie. Another explanation says incivility results from not having enough judges, arguing that incivility is bound to increase when there aren't enough judges to police legal practice. The first explanation assumes that "business" is inherently uncivilized, while the latter echoes the Law's stated belief that, left untended, people naturally revert to nastiness.

The problem with the stimulus/response analysis is that it tries to explain incivility as merely a result of external pressures. In many ways, the search for external causes of incivility mirrors a broader cultural trend of placing blame elsewhere. Psychology tells us that our personal inadequacies are responses to dysfunctional families (some even apply this meaningless concept to law firms); in politics some people argue for term limitations as the only way to prevent us from re-electing incumbents; in economics we hold foreign nations responsible for domestic shortcomings and assert that if only we had a balanced budget amendment we would be forced to do the right thing; and in society at large we accuse shadowy Drug Lords of being the cause of our national intoxication. Meanwhile, lawyers are blamed as the cause of everything from the litigation explosion to high health care costs. Blame is everywhere but here; with anyone but me.

A different approach to incivility begins to take shape when we remember that narrowly defining oneself in restrictive terms necessarily leads to the return of the repressed. Is it not possible that incivility erupts precisely because of the Law's obsessive desire to identify itself in terms of order and obedience? In other words, what if incivility is not a result of external influences but of an unduly limited self-definition?

"Civility" comes from roots that refer to citizenship and is related to other words referring to members of a household. Under these old meanings, being civilized means being good citizens and householders; to be uncivilized is to betray one's obligations to both society and home.

Being a good citizen might mean being better informed and more broadly involved, caring about what happens to the life of the polis. Viewed through the lens of civic responsibility, community concerns become indistinguishable from so-called individual ones. Perhaps one of the things incivility is pointing to is the need for the Law to be less concerned with imposing order and more involved with engendering a sense of shared community where values are embraced and lived intimately.

It isn't that the Law should be a profession and not a business, which would set up a false and unnecessary opposition between profession and business, but that it needs to be a better neighbor. But this cannot happen as long as the Law retains a defensive posture behind its obsession with order and obedience. When this happens the Law retreats within itself, becomes mean-spirited and short-tempered. You can almost hear the wagons circling. Ironically, when the Law does attempt to respond to incivility, it often does so with calls for more order and obedience, responses likely to guarantee just the opposite.

But there are other things going on here. When the Law says people don't respect it, that it is misunderstood, and that it needs to impose itself more forcefully onto people's lives, I hear talk laced with deep feelings of being cut off, detached, abandoned, disconnected. The very intensity with which the Law attempts to assert its control over society suggests that it currently feels left out, exiled. Note how often the people who make the laws seem to think they are above them; this is an example of how a preoccupation with order and obedience can split a person's perspective into a Me/Them outlook. Similarly, many lawyers complain of an amorphous lack of feeling, a sense of being anesthetized. Things are neither very good nor very bad, but just . . . mediocre. Passion fades, love becomes a parlor game, and inside we don't feel much at all. When this state of affairs reigns over the internal life of a profession or a person, it becomes prone to reaction instead of leadership, violent outbursts occur for no apparent reason, and transient values (order, obedience) replace fundamental ideals (justice, truth). Once the Law is cut off from its passions and forced to be a mere observer and organizer of life, it is just a matter of time before these repressed passions return to demand representation.

Incivility is a love disorder, not a result of working too many hours. We see this even more clearly when we remember some of the societal symptoms clustered nearby: the widespread belief that loyalty is eroding within the legal profession; the growth of an almost pathological individuality insisting that lawyers have to look out for number one because there is no security in relationships; the lingering feeling of emptiness despite material success; the break-up of long-standing partnerships; and the common lament that a life in the Law leaves no room for friends, family, other interests, or even oneself. All of these symptoms suggest that the Law feels divorced from the very society it is intended to serve.

Imposed obedience cannot rekindle the capacity to love. Rather, *incivility itself might be pointing the way by directing the Law to citizenship and householding,* both of which require attention, caring, and interest more than anything else. It is as if the Law is suffering from a lack of oxygen, that it needs air to fuel the combustion hidden in its heart. Moving into the world instead of being applied to it from without can provide this missing component. Everyday concerns, family affairs, matters of the heart— these are places for the Law to turn.

CHAPTER TWO
HOW THE LAW THINKS

WE START our search for the Law's constitutional themes by going to school. Law school, after all, is where people are taught to "think like a lawyer." Law school is where would-be lawyers first learn and practice the Law's fundamental values, attitudes, and beliefs. Law school reflects and perpetuates how the Law thinks, what it believes, and what it desires.

The process of "becoming a lawyer" includes more than learning strange language and a set of basic legal principles. At a deeper level it has to do with becoming acculturated to the legal mind, with learning how the legal perspective views things and how it prefers things to be. Somewhere along the line, law students go through a subtle, though radical, change. They begin to see things *in the first instance* through this legal mind set. Their very *perceptions* begin to be structured by assumptions provided by legal education. It is similar to becoming fluent in a foreign language. It is more than vocabulary, it has to do with instinctively feeling the rhythm of the language, entering it and hearing it talk. One friend told me he knew he was finally getting the hang of Spanish when he started dreaming in it. So too with becoming a lawyer—the entire world becomes a field where the legal mind is at play. The very nature of the mundane changes as everything is filtered through the perspectives of the legal mind. Everything becomes colored by law-tinted glasses.

A useful way of talking about these perspectives comes not from a psychologist but from Judge Learned Hand, who once referred to the "mental habits" that "indirectly determine" the legal profession. I take these mental habits to be the un-examined assumptions, myths, attitudes, ideas, and beliefs shaping both lawyer and profession; they comprise the legal profession's intellectual community and embody the legal mind's distinctive quality. Lawyers simply *see* things differently from other people, that's why they're lawyers. A therapist listening to an adulterer's tale will hear a different story than a divorce lawyer listening to the same account; more precisely put, the lawyer and the therapist are going to *hear* differently.

Saying such attitudes are "habitual" implies they are to some degree unconscious and involuntary. In archaic language, "habit" referred to a manner or custom of dress, and even earlier meant "to have or to hold." This means it is not so much we who have mental habits as they who have us, a reality familiar to anyone who has ever been had by a habit. Mental habits operate unconsciously and influence our daily thoughts and actions in ways that by definition we are unable to recognize. We are identified by the habits we wear.

GIVING PROCESS ITS DUE

A conflict often emerges early in law school when a law student's personal ideas about law and justice begin to come into contact with the attitudes and procedures of the Law as practiced professionally. Almost every lawyer can tell one or more anecdotes about a law professor saying something along the lines of "You are not here to find truth and justice, you are here to learn the Law." Early on, a professional distinction is drawn between justice as an altruistic goal and the Law's work-a-day procedures and practices. By the end of the second year of law school or so, explicit talk about fairness, justice, truth, and the like is rarely heard among either law professors or law students. Instead, such discussions become recast in terms of "due process" as the law student's focus increasingly becomes fixed on things procedural. To a freshly graduated lawyer, the exasperated lay person's remark that "It just doesn't seem fair" is a sure sign of someone unschooled in the Law. According to this rather paternalistic professional attitude, justice, truth, and fairness are fine for philosophical conversation, but are not practical or professional concerns of the first order.

Making a professional distinction between altruistic goals

and practical procedures is one way the Law deals with its own discomfort with altruism. The Law simply doesn't know what to do with Big Ideas that escape analytic definition. It knows that justice, truth, and fairness are supposed to be the end results of the legal process, but because such terms can't be defined in a way the Law is comfortable with it begins to shy away from direct contact with them. The Law's discomfort is understandable given its hunger for certainty and clarity and its strong predisposition in favor of fact-based argument over defined legal issues. But over time the Law's reluctance to engage the grand ideas at its heart *can limit and restrict the range of its imagination.* One of the most striking things to the non-lawyer who becomes involved in a lawsuit is the degree to which lawyers emphasize means more than ends, procedure more than outcome. I have heard many a person exclaim, after listening to a long explanation of the legal status of their claim, "What about what's right? Doesn't that have anything to do with it?" How does the Law respond? In the end, it seems to me, the ideals of justice and truth and the demands of procedural pragmatism must rely on one another. Lip service alone cannot sustain such an intimate and necessary relationship; what is required is mutual receptivity and respect.

Every field eventually runs into precisely this same discomfort over the meaning of its fundamental ideas and guiding metaphors. All founding and generative ideas are ambiguous—that is why they are founding and generative. No scientist can define "matter," no psychologist "soul" or "mind," no philosopher "wisdom." And so we shouldn't expect the Law to be able to define "justice." But the ability of a field to define its guiding metaphors is not as important as how it *imagines* these metaphors and the field's own relationship to them. This ongoing engagement sustains the life of the field and directly shapes its everyday practice. The greatest opportunities in any field unfold in the richness and diversity of its imagination.

III

In the Law's mind, the notion of due process connects the ideal of justice with the realistic necessities of administering justice in a tough and harried world. "Due process" refers to a more or less set system of rules, regulations, and procedures designed to ensure that disputes are dealt with in a reasonably similar fashion. "Notice" and "hearing" are pillars of due process, and upon these pillars rests a complex system of procedures designed to give all sides to a dispute fair opportunity to present their stories. Due process has proven to be a rich mine for the legal imagination; few legal ideas have been more protean than due process.

On the other hand, like any idea, due process is prone to excess and mistake. And, like any idea (or person for that matter), the very things that make it a strong idea contribute to the special nature of its weakness. For example, due process believes that if we do things over and over in the same way then we should get the same, or at least similar, results—a belief that ties in nicely with the Law's associated desire for uniformity of result. But if taken too far or too literally, this belief can lead to procedural myopia, bureaucratic entrenchment, and impersonalized justice.

Procedures, whether in the laboratory or the courtroom, are designed to restrict and control variables. If variables can be held constant, and if the same procedures are repeated exactly from one time to the next, then the expectation is that we should get the same result. But this regularity is exactly the source of many of the problems associated with due process. The ability to repeat an experiment with uniform results might be a necessary component of scientific verification, and one that is approachable in the confines of the laboratory; but the same degree of uniformity cannot be achieved in the legal context precisely because life is not a laboratory. Life is too complex, personalities too quirky, and events too unforeseeable to satisfy the scientist's strict criteria. Once life is viewed as a group of variables, there will invariably be too many to control. This is not a criticism of due process, but merely an example of how every idea, every psychological perspective, every mental habit has limitations and casts a necessary shadow.

Due process implies an ontological outlook. It implies deep assumptions about how the world holds together, how things work, the natural order of things. Just as the scientific method presupposes a consistent and governed world, so due process assumes the world is, if not intrinsically ordered, at least *amenable* to order. Due process ultimately believes that order can be established in even the most chaotic situations if only enough procedural safeguards can be ensured, and that if surprise and uncertainty can be minimized then over time things will balance themselves out in predictable ways. These beliefs sustain due process, but they also are the source of its anxiety. Due process feels threatened when experience refuses to comport with its theories. As with any idea or person, due process becomes anxious and reactionary when it meets the limits of its own ontological implications.

THE SCALES AND THE SWORD

Law is full of overt symbolism. Two of these symbols have been especially enduring: the scales and the sword. The scales are usually taken to represent an approach to justice based on impartial balancing and weighing of evidence. The sword suggests that force and the threat of force are essential attributes for justice.

The scales and the sword influence and support many of the Law's ideas. We have just noted how due process contents itself with its shortcomings through the promise that everything will eventually "balance out." Very early on, law students learn that different kinds of cases require different "burdens of proof." In a criminal context, for example, the prosecution has the burden of proving its case "beyond a reasonable doubt," while in civil cases, the baseline standard of proof is a "preponderance of the evidence." Lawyers and judges often explain this concept by saying that one side has to show their position is "more likely than not." We can almost see the scales tipping one way or the other. Very often, in fact, lawyers will literally invoke the scales before a jury by pantomiming them with up-turned and weighing palms. The metaphorical influence of the scales on the legal imagination ranges from the grand—teaching that individual liberties must be balanced against broader social concerns—to the everyday, as when lawyers rely on "balancing tests" that weigh competing circumstances to guide legal analysis.

The sword advances the belief that force is necessary for Law. Indeed, the legal mind itself has a cutting, piercing, double-edgeness to it. Law students and lawyers are encouraged to "hone" their legal skills and to "sharpen" their arguments. In analyzing fact patterns, students are taught to split them into component parts and then to consider each dissected entity separately. A legal argument is made up of "points" to be "driven home." Courts often formulate legal tests that have "prongs." In negotiations, one hears of "splitting the difference" or, in a more direct reference to Solomonic decision-making, of "splitting the baby." A popular complaint about lawyers is that they "split hairs." And the more violent, vengeful qualities of the sword show up repeatedly in the Law's adversarial, warrior-like demeanor.

You get the picture. The dovetailing between the Law's symbols and its recurring mental habits is not coincidental. It is further demonstration that imagination is essential to how we think. Of special significance is that the scales and sword simply *feel* so right. They are so much a part of our image of law and justice that they feel more than appropriate, they feel downright *necessary.*

OBJECTIVITY AND THE CASE METHOD

The classical western depiction of Justice shows her as blindfolded. Not blind, mind you, but blindfolded. This usually is taken to mean that to reach a just decision we must close our eyes to bias, prejudice, and passion—all of which endanger fairness and impartiality. In more conceptual terms, this means that we must be "objective." The Law is continuously striving for objectivity.

A little word-history. "Objective" is based on the word "object," which originally meant "to throw before or against," or "oppose." These old meanings are reflected in the modern use of an "objection" to a line of questioning, a legal argument, or a piece of evidence. These old meanings also are at work when we teach law students to cast the facts of a case against a legal backdrop to examine them for their legal significance. Before advocacy must come objectivity, and taking an objective view of the facts means first taking them as objects of study. Objectifying facts allows the legal mind to sort out those that are irrelevant to the legal issues at hand while accentuating others that support or oppose a particular legal position.

The step of organizing a given set of facts into a "case" is central to the legal mind-set and is among the first things law students learn. I remember when I first became consciously aware of this process. I was in a criminal law class and we were studying a rape case. A student had recited the facts of the case and the court's holding, and the professor was leading us through the "elements" of the crime of rape. As we went through the legal requirements for establishing a rape case, I suddenly realized something was being left out. The horror was missing. The violence and brutality of this particular human tragedy had been replaced by an intellectual exercise. There was even a kind of gamesmanship quality about the discussion ("how to prove penetration?") that itself betrayed a repression of the *actual* facts of the case. It reminded me of how grave diggers and coroners joke about death.

Objectivity can have an anesthetizing effect on the lawyer's soul. Through the case method, objectivity translates visceral human experiences into schemata so they might be more easily compared to other "like cases." In many ways, this process of separating and categorizing facts for the sake of comparison mimics the scientific method with its emphasis on analysis and categories. Just think how much the law digest system with its headnotes and indices reminds one of a biology text with its families, genera, and species.

In both law and science, objectivity's preferred approach is analytic and its preferred analytic tools are abstraction and rationality. Abstraction and rationality are the intellectual workhorses of "objectivity." They are the means by which objectivity works, and, as means, are instructive as to the ends objectivity seeks.

Abstraction means "to draw away from," while "rationality" connotes "computation, sum, or number." Abstraction contributes to objectivity's anesthetizing effect by drawing the lawyer away from the case, on the one hand offering an overview's broader perspective, while at the same time allowing the lawyer to resist becoming "overly involved" in the case. Viewed through an abstracting lens, involvement and objectivity are seen as inversely proportionate; the closer we get, the less objective we become. The answer, says abstraction, is to get a little distance, to avoid "losing sight" of a case by getting "wrapped up" in it, to not let the trees blind us to the forest, and so on. Lawyers are taught to abjure representing friends and relatives precisely on this point, because of a concern that familiarity and affection might cloud the lawyer's objectivity. The Law has even codified its fear that there are conflicts in interest.

Rationality has strong mathematical overtones, and therefore it is no accident that disciplines which embrace rationality as a primary method seek first to reduce things to discrete, unvarying entities. Rationality reflects objectivity's penchant both for dividing (the sword again) and comparing (the scales). And so it isn't surprising, even if it is disappointing, that some lawyers and judges struggle to apply quantifiable means like cost/benefit analyses as substitutes for more humane legal analysis.

We have already pointed to objectivity's anesthetizing effects. But I also suspect that when objectivity is taken too far it contributes to the Law's feelings of being misunderstood, overworked, and isolated. What does objectivity feel like from within? What are its psychological dimensions? If the stories I hear from lawyers in therapy and the results of numerous studies of lawyers are any indication, objectivity feels like isolation, and its encasing attitudes can leave a person feeling rigid and stiff. Again and again in therapy, lawyers talk about their daydreams of breaking free from the daily grind, of going crazy, doing something wild and unpredictable; but then they catch themselves and withdraw within the narrow boundaries of their objectified self-image. It is as if the *lawyer* is transformed into an object— cold, heartless, dead. Pressure builds. Anxiety (which some psychologists define as a kind of self-contained stress) increases. Finally, something "snaps" or "cracks" and the lawyer "breaks under the strain."

There is a dramatic rise in psychological disturbances among law students during their law school years. Depending on the particular symptom, law students are almost four times more likely than the general population to suffer from depression and anxiety. The usual reason given is that law students are under a lot of stress, which is sort of like saying fire burns you because it's hot. But what if there is something else too? A pioneering study on the psychological effects of legal education concluded that

> [Law] students learn to depend on [dialectical] skills to provide solutions to many and different real problems in life. . . . An orderly process of weighing and interpreting many life events results. The analytic experience is made easier by the fact that the entire process and result is impersonalized and viewed largely from an intellectual context. *So far as the experiencing of problems, particularly other persons' problems, is made completely impersonal, the development of legal skills is reassuring. At the same time, these may not reach and probably do not touch upon*

the psychological sore-points that create anxiety for the individual student-lawyer.[1] (Italics mine.)

Do you hear what has happened? Objectivity is a double-edged sword, on one hand "reassuring" the law student of his or her ability to deal with human problems on an analytic level, while at the same time failing to touch the student's growing anxiety. Elevating objectivity to a way of life and the elevation of psychological distress among law students and lawyers go hand in hand. As we saw in the Law's obsession with order and obedience, psychological problems arise when one idea or perspective tyrannizes all others, thereby restricting the soul's imaginative versatility. When objective criteria become the only ways in which the Law is allowed to imagine, then the Law has fallen victim to psychological dogmatism. Categories become imperative.

Here we come to another reading of Justice's blindfold. It isn't only passion or prejudice that the blindfold obscures, but perception itself. Justice can no longer look out upon the world, can no longer appreciate its subtle variations and delicate distinctions. Instead, the blindfold turns vision inward so that Justice's struggle to comprehend reality becomes necessarily solipsistic. Of course Justice must "see" things in its own terms—that is all that is left it. Memories of how things looked before the blindfold begin to fade as the out of sight becomes out of mind. Abstractions, idealized systems, and coldly objectified facts replace sensory awareness, and gone from view are all chances for shared vision. With blinders in place, "I don't see your point" comes to mean, "I cannot look through your eyes."

A SIDEBAR ON STRESS

This is a good place to put the whole question of stress in perspective.

Robert Kugelmann, a psychologist who has done groundbreaking work on stress, reminds us that "stress" was originally an *engineering* term. It had to do with roads, bridges, metallurgy, and the like. In its early usage it was confined to "physical . . . pressure or tension exerted upon a material object,"[2] a meaning still common among engineers and others involved with the mechanical arts. It was not until the onset of the industrial revolution that "stress" began to be applied to human beings, and not until the 1930s that it gained currency as a psychological term.

Stress requires a style of imagining that sees psychological life in terms of material objects. This materialistic bias is the preferred stance of modern science, a stance also dedicated, ironically enough, to the belief that material objects are soulless. Despite this denial of soul, it is interesting how psychology, in its rush to be accepted as a science, has wholeheartedly, if not always wittingly, embraced this materialistic bias. When modern psychology talks about stress, it usually talks in terms like "dynamics," "coping mechanisms," "hardiness," "adaptation," or "relaxation techniques." Popular prescriptions for "relieving stress" include "working out" stress through exercise, as if relief lay in a harder body, or in monitoring brain waves through "bio-feedback." The theme in these responses is that stress is a structural defect best corrected through controlling and relieving pressure.

Although these various materialistic prescriptions might alleviate the physical symptoms of stress (tight neck, headaches, rock-hard shoulders), they do little to respond to the underlying psychological attitudes that create and sustain stress to begin with. They are simply too mechanical, too reductive. It's as if those who prescribe them believe we can relieve stress through purely physical means or through sheer force of will. But such ideas actually reinforce (more engineering talk) stress and can even create situations where the means meant to reduce stress actually increase it.

The dominant theme in almost all modern methods for "reducing" stress is management. "Stress management" has become something of a growth industry, with consultants nationwide coaching individuals and groups in how to reduce stress. Recommendations range from learning better time-management skills, achieving more balance between professional and personal commitments, increased use of alternative methods for resolving legal disputes, flexible work schedules, and so on. The message in all of these approaches is the same: Stress is just one more hard indicia of modern life that must be addressed, along with things like crime, environmental degradation, and social inequality, all of which are seen as themselves stress inducing.

Most stress management techniques are useful and effective. The sheer enjoyment of a massage or the invigoration of a brisk walk after being stuck in an office all day can hardly be denied. But there's a piece missing in these managerial approaches. The fact is you can meditate in the morning, jog in the afternoon, and manage all your time in between and still not touch the underlying sense of stress in daily life. After all, isn't there something stressful in being told we must "manage" our stress? It seems no matter how much stress we "work out" there is more where it came from.

Stress cannot exist without our first likening ourselves unto machines. If a bridge is under stress from having too much weight on it, you either reduce the weight on the bridge or find ways to make the bridge stronger—exactly the same approaches espoused by mainstream stress management techniques. Either we reduce the factors adding to our stress or find ways to reinforce our load-bearing capacities. Otherwise, we risk blowing a gasket, popping a vein, snapping, cracking, or breaking under the strain, burning out, crashing, collapsing, or caving in to pressure.

But we are not bridges, or machines, or even computers. Nor are we in any essential way "like machines" or "like computers." And yet we persist in such talk while remaining surprised at how stressed we feel. Such modern metaphors might have literary value, but they cannot encompass the human soul. The problem is that after a while we forget they *are* metaphors and begin to think of ourselves literally in such mechanistic terms, thereby increasing our feelings of stress by over-stressing metaphors that were never meant to carry such a heavy burden. Here we come to the heart of things, because it is this dehumanizing philosophical undercurrent that sustains stress.

Kugelmann is right when he theorizes that "only a people living in an age of science can *experience* stress."[3] Philosopher Sam Keen is right when he concludes that stress "is a product, not of an excess of fire, but of a deficiency of passion."[4] Both point to the fact that stress is as much a philosophical disorder as it is the result of this or that personal or environmental factor; it implicates our deepest imaginings about ourselves and the world. Any truly psychological approach to stress must therefore entail a shift in consciousness that reaffirms the deep and sympathetic connection between oneself and the world. Otherwise no amount of meditation, maintenance, or management can help.

Another way of looking at stress is to recognize that *stress and*

objectivity require one another. Both operate on similar philosophical assumptions about the nature of things, stress seeing everything in terms of "pressure exerted upon a material object,"
while objectivity must turn experiences into lifeless objects it
can manipulate and organize (the "rape case" phenomenon).
Both need objects on which to work.

Given their philosophical affinity, it isn't surprising that
stress and objectivity have similar psychological implications.
Both are typified by a hardness and brittleness of spirit. Both reduce our sense of vitality and flexibility. Both are prone to over-
work. And both anesthetize our sensual connection to the
greater world. In fact, perhaps stress indicates that objectivity,
not us, is what's being overworked, that we are expecting too
much from it, and that it is not getting enough time off.

This is a particularly difficult problem for the Law because of
its near total embrace of objectivity as a defining method and its
obsession with order and obedience. It is interesting to note how
many of the usual remedies given for stress involve turning one's
attention away from the alleged stress-inducing event (take a vacation, meditate, go to the gym, close your eyes and concentrate
on relaxing, etc.), all of which are examples of how objectivity
uses its abstracting talents to avoid direct emotional involvement. In turn, order and obedience create an atmosphere of false
stability that allows objectivity's lack of passion to go unchal-
lenged. But when things go out of whack, as they inevitably do,
this *quid pro quo* becomes an engine of stress. The Law reacts to
unexpected change the only way it allows itself to react: it bears
down and works even harder to be more objective and to create
new procedures to restore order. The only way to stop the engine
is either to eliminate change, which seems unlikely, or to cut off
the engine's fueling assumptions.

When objectivity is internalized, we start to imagine ourselves as objects acting within a "system" designed to maintain
order and ensure obedience. We then almost certainly begin to
experience stress. Of course there are "too many things to do."
Of course there is "too little time." Of course we start spending
less time outside of the system, taking fewer vacations and worrying about things back at the system when we do, or working
too much because we fear that without us things will get out of
hand, pile up, overload, fall through the cracks, go haywire. And
of course anxiety builds as we come to think that as mere objects

in a system we ourselves can always be replaced. The psy
of the objectivity-order-obedience trinity dictates these feel

LIFE BEGINS AT LAW SCHOOL

Getting back to what the Law wants and how these wants
manifest themselves in law school, I have been increasingly
struck by the "life begins at law school" syndrome. The symptoms of this syndrome are familiar to every law student past his
or her first year, every lawyer, and everyone who knows someone who has gone to law school. The primary symptom of this
syndrome is a kind of amnesia or mental block about life before
law school.

I once gave a talk to a group of lawyers and judges whose
median level of legal experience was around fifteen years. The
topic of the talk was some of the myths that influence how lawyers imagine themselves as professionals, and we talked a good
bit about the ancient origins of some of our modern legal ideas.
There was a reception afterwards, and a number of people came
up to me and said things like "I was a classics major in college,
but I never thought about myths having anything to do with the
law" or "I used to read a lot of English literature, and when you
said such-and-such I was reminded about this one passage in
Dickens."

Other stories come from people who have friends going
through law school. Almost invariably, these people talk about
how the lawyer-in-training is changing. Common observations:
the law student is becoming more argumentative over the least
little thing, almost seeming to look for a chance to argue; they
have become a little haughty, assuming an air of superiority;
they seem older, as if they are trying to affect a range of experience beyond their years; or they simply aren't as much fun to be
around as they used to be. On the other side, lawyers and law
students, if asked, routinely tell about all the friends they never
see any more.

The simple fact is that there appears to be something about
law school that disconnects people from the life they had before
law school. When I talk to experienced lawyers who spend a lot
of time teaching new lawyers the ropes, they very often tell me
how hard it is to get new lawyers to look at a problem in non-
legal terms. It's as if new lawyers are unable to connect their law

hology

gs.

47

ie vast range of experience they acquired
nehow, legal training usurps this experi-
ng it altogether or by insisting it be re-
ore amenable to the legal mind-set. At its
at law school syndrome encourages an ar-
ic attitude that assumes a legal response to
r to non-legal responses.

nows a lawyer or someone who is becoming
a la..., kind of arrogance being pointed to. "Well,
you have to consider all the possibilities," says the second-year
law student to his fifty-five year-old parent. The tone is one of
polite indulgence, as if the parent is a bit of a mope, hopelessly
naïve, unworldly, and simply unaware of how things work. The
haughtiness belies a belief that the legal perspective is the "true"
perspective, the "real world" perspective. The law student is doing his best to sound like *he* is the parent; you can hear it in his
forced caution. Circumspection replaces youthful idealism. All
is calm, wizened advice. The irony, of course, is that the law
student is completely unaware of his conduct and actually is
demonstrating the effects of a stalled maturation. After all, true
experience *increases* the range of one's responses, it doesn't limit
a person to the party line.

III

In tribal cultures, at some point in a young person's life he or
she is expected to go through a series of initiatory ritual experiences that transform him or her into an adult member of the
tribe. Generally speaking, anthropologists describe initiation as
having three phases: separation, transition, and incorporation.
In phase one, initiates are separated from their family and are
required to go through various rituals as a means of leaving behind their former lives as children. In the second phase, they are
introduced to the mysteries of adulthood and what it means to
be full member of the tribe. Sacred stories are told, often including the creation myths of the tribe itself, and other acts are taken
to cement the initiate's bond with the essential life of the tribe.
Lastly, the initiates are re-introduced to the tribe in their new
standing as fully participating members. Acceptance of the initiates by the tribe is universal; everyone who completes the
ritual initiation is welcomed back into the tribe.

Two things stand out when we compare this traditional initiatory pattern with the process of "becoming a lawyer" via law school. First, initiation is available to *all* members of the tribe. True, boys and girls might go through different rites, but the initiatory experience itself is available to all members of the tribe without exception and without need of any particular qualifications. Second, the end result of initiation is the incorporation of *all* initiates into the tribe. In other words, initiation does not result in a young person being segregated from the tribe but just the opposite. Through initiation, the young person moves out into the larger world of the tribal environment, becoming connected to it in ways unimagined before the initiation.

Compare these initiatory rituals to law school. Despite the fact that some people talk about law school as a rite of passage, there are glaring and significant differences. To start with, law school is not something all members of the tribe go through. I don't mean law schools are inherently discriminatory, although there is evidence to support this view, but simply that not everyone in the tribe goes through law school. People have to *qualify* for law school through LSAT scores, grades, references, and what not. But most important, the law school experience does not perform the function of opening the law school graduate to the larger world. Instead, after graduation the new lawyer is welcomed, not into society at large, but into a subset of society, a profession. Law school is not an initiatory experience but one of *induction*. Lawyers become "insiders," part of what is best characterized as a fraternal organization, complete with membership dues, special language, and a subculture of courts and legal processes.

Although legal training performs the first phase of initiation, that of separation, it then veers from the initiatory pattern by beginning *to limit rather than expand the lawyer's sense of broadbased community.* The results are familiar to anyone who has been in or observed other groups of inductees. Although infighting might occur, a fierce loyalty nonetheless develops within the group *vis à vis* those not in the group. (I have heard more than one lawyer refer to non-lawyers as "civilians.") The group is likely to develop ideas and practices designed to accentuate and glamorize its separateness while ensuring its continued existence as a closed order. Rigidity and bureaucracy become problematic as the order establishes its own ways for doing everything. (Within the group, these highly stylized practices are accepted as necessary for maintaining the group's internal security, and even become carriers of great nostalgia.) Revealing internal secrets to outsiders becomes a cardinal sin, and criticizing the group in front of outsiders borders on outright treason.

The life begins at law school syndrome is one consequence of this cloistered mentality. Because non-legal experiences cannot help but remind the lawyer of his or her broader connections to the world beyond the Law, such experiences, like bad recruits, must be drummed out.

THE CULT OF INDIVIDUALISM

The scene is familiar. The crusty-but-brilliant law professor calls on a hapless law student to recite the facts of a case. First there is silence, then the silence becomes uncomfortably long. At last comes the meek reply that the student has not read the case.

"Well then," purrs the professor with all the warmth of a tiger preparing to pounce, "we'll just read it together. Stand up, Mr. Jones."

What follows is akin to a public flogging, as poor Mr. Jones is made to stand up and display his ignorance in front of the entire class. But ask the professor why he or she subjected Mr. Jones to such embarrassment and at some point you are likely to be told that it was to make Mr. Jones stronger, to teach him that lawyers often have to "wing it," and that part of being an effective lawyer is the ability to never let them see you sweat. Underneath this veneer of pedantry is a powerful message: For a lawyer to admit ignorance is to admit weakness, and to admit weakness is to open oneself to attack. People who are close to lawyers can attest to the depth of this training and often comment how rare it is to hear a lawyer admit to not knowing something. Lawyers are taught to bluff, expected to bluff. Lawyers must always give the impression of knowledge and confidence, must always know.

This kind of training creates a cult of individualism that leaves lawyers no way out. Expected to be forever self-sufficient, strong, knowing, aggressive, and confident, the lawyer is expected to be more than human. Even in situations where one would expect to find communal effort and collegiality—say in a law firm or among a group of lawyers representing the same client—we see the cult of individualism at work, transforming collegiality into competition and community into a mere collection of "I's."

Many of the mental habits taught in law school promote a distorted and burdensome sense of individuality. Certainly the objective mind-set described above, with its preference for discrete, clearly defined entities, fits nicely into this style of individualism. But combine this objective coldness with the constant circumspection and caution with which lawyers are taught to face the world, and you have an overwhelming combination that closes the lawyer in on himself or herself. Add the unspoken but clearly conveyed sense of aristocracy that law school encourages and you have a prescription for an alienated profession made up of lonely men and women.

But the basic problem is that the style of individuality taught in law school is false individuality. At base it has little if anything to do with individuality as a psychological reality. *From the perspective of soul, individuality has to do with uniqueness and eccentricity, not self-confident isolation.* That lawyers *as a group* display this kind of in-your-face individualism is proof that this kind of individuality is conformism masquerading as individuality.

For once, the reason for this false individuality appears fairly straightforward. The Law has already said that without rules anarchy necessarily follows. No wonder the Law therefore wants to limit expressions of true individuality. The true individual, one who has a sense of his or her own uniqueness, is perceived as a potential danger to the established order. In the movies the rebellious cop eventually has to take matters into his own hands, tossing the badge in the drawer and tucking another gun under his belt. We are at once fascinated and disturbed by such characters precisely because they have the courage of their convictions, a courage that leads them to act "outside the Law." But from the Law's perspective they must be seen as loose cannon, vigilantes, and sources of disruption.

The Law wants people to act as the Law says, not as their personal *daimones* suggest. Individuality will necessarily transgress social norms as long as it is imagined as the *alternative* to community. In addition, the false individuality taught in law school stresses a unitary and consistent personality. Probably this is a direct reflection of the Law's broader demands for uniformity and consistency. But in any event it discourages an appreciation of our eccentricities and an affirmation of our inherent multiplicity.

In a curious but potentially dangerous alliance, modern psychology often perpetuates the very kind of pathological individuality being taught under the rubric of the Law. Self-esteem, personal growth, getting it together, owning one's emotions, becoming centered, finding harmony, fitting in, being well-related—all of these catch-phrases of modern psychology have as part of their construct a fundamental mistrust of the unique craziness that makes each of us what we are. In our heart of hearts, we know we are "different," that nobody else sees things quite like we do, and that there is an extent to which we can never really express to another person the mysterious something that makes us who we are. It is in our intimate familiarity with our Secret Selves that our individuality truly resides, and yet it is precisely those feelings that both Law and modern psychology wish to eradicate. In fact, the vast majority of self-help movements can actually be seen as an arm of the Law, working underground to put down rebellious outbursts and to smooth things over into nice, homogeneous, bland mediocrity.

That the Law has to work so hard at instilling self-confidence in its emissaries makes one wonder just how confident the Law is in itself. For all its talk about individual rights and freedoms, the Law appears to harbor deep concerns about the inherent volatility of individuality. The Law loves to recite the classic example of the person who cries "Fire" in a crowded theater as a way of showing that, in the end, individuality must succumb to social control. But what are the psychological implications of approaching individuality with an eye ever watchful for trouble? What does it mean to the life of the soul when social order is elevated to divine status? Do we not weaken the soul's vitality when we replace heart-felt faith in individuality with expectations of conformity? Just think how hard it is for both Law and psychology to acknowledge weakness, vulnerability, quirkiness, and uncertainty as *essential* to our deepest individuality.

THE LAW AND THE WORD

Nothing more readily identifies a lawyer than his or her language. Although legal language probably is more accessible and understandable now than ever before, it still retains a fondness for "aforesaids," "wheretofores," and obscure Latin phrases. But what is especially interesting is not so much legal language's arcane remnants, but the particular ways in which the Law views language.

The lawyer has been married to the word from the very beginning. The earliest lawyers in ancient Greece were speechwriters who prepared scripts for litigants to recite before the court. Because it was thought bad form for litigants to have others speak on their behalf, the lawyer carried out this speechwriting in secret. In those rare instances that a lawyer did appear on behalf of a litigant, it was as an interested friend whose appearance was assumed to mean the lawyer personally believed in the litigant's character and cause. Only later did the lawyer emerge as an "objective" tactician and advisor, but even then these functions were subordinate to the lawyer's primary role as *logographer* or "word-writer."

In modern legal practice, the connection between the lawyer's personal belief in a cause and the words used by the lawyer in advocating that cause has been severed. Indeed, one of the things fanning public distrust of lawyers is the belief that although a lawyer might display a facile use of words, we cannot assume the lawyer believes what he or she is saying. And of course at some level this often is an accurate perception. One of the things hammered into law students is that personal conviction in a cause, although perhaps desirable, is not necessary for legal representation. The lawyer's job in modern society is to articulate the client's cause in the most persuasive manner possible, regardless of the lawyer's personal feelings about that cause.

The deeper question, the psychological question, is What happens to the lawyer when he or she internalizes this distinction between his or her personal beliefs and the word? What happens when one habitually listens to oneself saying things one doesn't believe? Who's left to trust then? I mean, if we can't trust our own voice whose can we trust? Two of the more common results of this situation are an abiding fear of the word and a sense of personal dissociation.

As any trial lawyer can tell you, one of the greatest anxieties of trial practice comes when the client takes the stand. Despite all of the coaching and practice, "Who knows what they might say?" The lawyer is anxious because he or she knows words often say things we don't intend and reveal secrets we desperately want to keep hidden. Despite concerted efforts to control the words coming from a witness, every lawyer knows that words will constantly confound such efforts. Words seem to have a life of their own, to want to tell their own stories, and reveal their own secrets. From Freudian slips to asking one question too many in a cross-examination, words seem determined to speak their own minds.

Similar situations exist in every facet of legal practice. Whether it is drafting a demand letter, a motion, a brief, a settlement agreement, a contract, or whatever, the lawyer goes to incredible lengths to craft "air-tight" language. An essential ingredient in "good" legal writing is the ability to confine certain words to precise meanings while leaving others purposely ambiguous. (Of course, even ambiguity must be confined to its desired place.) To accomplish this task, the Law has developed a highly specialized language that seeks to excise metaphor, simile, and image. From the Law's perspective, all of these are seen as fraught with ambiguity, multiple meanings, and uncertainty. But there is more going on here than an innocent quest for precision. The Law is extraordinarily concerned about the damage words can do. Lawyers worry about "loose" language and spend hours trying to eliminate loop-holes, agonizing over the possibility that the wrong word might "come back to haunt them" down the road. The ghost in the word.

All of this would be mere semantics if the results were not so devastating. Elsewhere in the history of our culture, the Word has been said to have divine origins, and even to carry within it the power of creation itself. If in the beginning there is the Word, what happens when the Law tries to cut off the Word's generative capabilities? This religious, mythical background would suggest that by trying to limit the Word we also are trying to limit the divine's inherent creativity as expressed in the spontaneity of language. When lawyers attempt to exorcise the ghost within the word, they betray their own psychological depths. Words give life and soul, and if we want a varied and rich soul-life we must have a varied and rich language. To continue the analogy a step further, when we try to strip words of their inherent multiplicity of meaning we risk becoming the Devil's

Advocate, estranged and alienated, an outcast fated to cold isolation and loneliness. Make no mistake, loss of the Word is loss of soul.

We all know that people in intimate relationships don't communicate on the basis of carefully articulated rational ideas. Rather, such relationships depend on indirection and metaphor, of saying one thing when something else is intended and then depending on mutual experience and empathy of the partners to sense the connection. This conflict in communicative styles often erupts in therapy: "Why can't he just say what he means!" demands the lawyer, when in fact the non-lawyer *is* saying precisely what he means, only in the native tongue of the soul, a tongue depending on multiple shades of meaning best apprehended through imagination and intuition. Unfortunately, the Law's objective mind-set often considers such language unintelligible and demands it be translated into "rational" discourse. But from the soul's perspective, such translation means killing the word, giving up the ghost. And so an impasse is reached. Unable or unwilling to understand, the lawyer is left confused and frustrated, losing his or her ability to listen, watching bewildered as another friendship fades away, a spouse becomes a stranger, a child is abandoned. At its worst, the demand that the soul relinquish its language separates the lawyer from his or her own soul—the ultimate abandonment.

Quite apart from the psychological toll on the lawyer, words themselves suffer when they are detached from their intrinsic creativity and spontaneity (the latter being the very thing the trial lawyer fears most). When detached from themselves in this manner, words become a kind of parody of communication, unable to convey meaning any more than sound can carry in a vacuum. Eventually, words rebel in a desperate attempt to re-establish contact with the living. They erupt in unexpected outbursts. Documents and testimony get longer and longer as it takes more words to express a simple idea, and what starts as a trickle suddenly becomes an unstemmable torrent of impassioned words. When words become devalued and debased they are spent as freely as water—words, words, words.

People will continue to complain about "legalese" and the lawyer's apparent unwillingness to speak "normal" language. But my point is a different one. After all, the poet or the novelist shares the lawyer's desire for exactly the right word. Nor is there anything inherently wrong with jargon—within a discipline there is much to be said for a professional shorthand that encourages precise understanding and communication. Problems arise when the Law becomes afraid of the Word because of the Word's inherent multiplicity of meaning. It is one thing to craft a sentence to convey a precise meaning; it is quite another to reduce language to a kind of pseudo-mathematics where metaphorical depth and imaginative power are denied and suppressed.

CHAPTER THREE
HOW THE LAW WORKS

LAW SCHOOL introduces the Law's basic mental habits. The legal profession then provides the ongoing daily structures that sustain and perpetuate these habits. Just as we can learn much about people from how they work, so too the legal profession's preferences in how it organizes itself are instructive in revealing the Law's underlying beliefs and attitudes. What kind of organizations does the Law construct? How does it classify its workers into organizational niches? How does it think about the time it spends at work? How does it relate work to the rest of life?

These are huge questions, and our purpose isn't to chart all of the Law's organizational tendencies. Instead let us dip our cups into the Law's stream of consciousness and take a close look at the samples we pull up.

ORDER AND ORGANIZATION

The most obvious and dominant characteristic of how the Law is organized is *hierarchy*. The legal profession is designed along vertical lines—from the judicial system with its lower to higher courts, to law firms with support staff at the bottom and rain-making senior partners at the top, to corporate law departments that easily accept the hierarchical organization given with corporate life. In each of these instances there is a clear and consistent pattern that more authority is invested the higher one goes.

What psychological assumptions underlie this hierarchical pattern and flow from it? First, it seems to me that investing greater authority in higher places mirrors a cultural belief that with height and distance comes perspective. One reason we trust higher courts and senior partners to make fundamental policy decisions is that we believe they are "in a better position" to do so. They get the big picture. Conversely, the lower down the ladder you go, the more narrow the range of decision-making authority.

The idea that height gives more perspective fits nicely into the Law's preference for objectivity and abstraction. Distance avoids the clouding influences of personal involvement, emotion, or prejudice. The bird's-eye view is preferred to ground-level engagement. The higher we get, the more of an overview we are allowed; by seeing the big picture we can more easily fit together the various pieces of the puzzle. Just think how commanding generals have always sought out higher ground so they could sense the overall patterns of the battlefield. Whether this means finding the highest hill, or having the latest satellite photographs, the importance of this kind of intelligence is undeniable.

The downside of this belief, of course, is the risk that getting too far above the fray will divorce us from details that are of ultimate concern to the frontline troops. The general might see the sweep of history but neglect the need for sturdy shoes and warm blankets. This is an inherent problem of hierarchy—it inhibits communication, especially from the ground up. Just how much does the senior partner in the corner office know about conditions in the mail room? And even if the partner wanted to know, how would he or she go about finding out? One answer might be to ask the supervisor of the mail room. Another might be to call a meeting of everyone in the mail room and have the partner attend. Some information could be obtained in either case, but we all know much would go unsaid, most likely the very things the partner really needs to know. Like pulled taffy, hierarchies tend to bunch up at the ends while thinning, and weakening, at the middle.

III

A religious tenet of wide belief is that Power Rests On High. Given this belief, few people on the lower rungs are going to risk an encounter with Higher Authority. (This belief also contributes to so called "empowerment" problems within hierarchies.

People in the mail room will never feel like they have power within the organization as long as we culturally embrace the belief that Power Rests On High.) Sometimes it gets to the point that both ends of the spectrum believe they are different from one another—qualitatively different in ways going beyond the hierarchy to more constitutional matters. Hierarchy produces aristocratic prejudice.

When I first started working in a law firm, I was a docket clerk. A docket clerk is a person who travels back and forth to the courts to make various filings, to get routine information from court files, and the like. In the organizational scheme of things, a docket clerk is much closer to the mail room than to the corner office. Later, after law school, I became a lawyer at the same firm where I had been a docket clerk. It was then I noticed an unusual phenomenon. Before, when I was a docket clerk, some lawyers in the office would pass me in the hall without acknowledgment. Then, once I became a lawyer, these same lawyers were suddenly nodding and saying, "Good morning." Curious. Even more curious, a similar event did not occur from the other direction. The support staff still said hello to me after I became a lawyer just as they had before.

Now here is an example of how hierarchy's aristocratic tendencies can produce the exact opposite of what the hierarchy intends. Instead of expanding their vision from their vantage points higher up the ladder, the offending lawyers had actually narrowed their personal perspective. Perhaps they were just snobs, or simply ill-mannered despite their pretensions. But over time I have noticed that hierarchy seems almost naturally to work at cross-purposes with itself. It often contradicts its own belief that the higher one gets the broader one's perspective becomes.

We could say this contradiction is really a social matter, one of a pervasive caste mentality that ignorantly makes determinations of personal worth according to organizational status. But that begs the question. The critical thing to realize is that these hierarchical tendencies are connected to the Law's deeper preferences for objectivity and abstraction. Hierarchies depend on both for their existence. This can be seen graphically by looking at an organizational chart, whether of a court system, a law firm, or a corporate department. There, in the boxes and connecting lines, is a visual representation of the phenomenon we are talking about. Boxes and Lines—that is how the objective and abstracting mind works, categorizing things according to some predetermined plan, and allowing communication only along official lines.

But what happens when people get boxed in, their minds and imaginations held within four corners and bounded by solid lines of defense? Perhaps the Lawyers who didn't say good morning to the Docket Clerk were not rude people so much as they were unable to *perceive* the Docket Clerk because he was outside the Lawyers' box, shielded from view, irrelevant, invisible. Talking in the hallway did not fall along established lines of communication between the categories. Only when the Docket Clerk became a Lawyer did he suddenly become visible.

But wait a second. If that's the case, then how come I continued to be visible to the other people whose boxes I had left? Once again, the organizational chart provides a possible clue. The higher we go in a hierarchy, the smaller the number of people represented by the boxes. When we say "higher-ups" constitute an "exclusive" group, we are being precisely correct. "Exclusivity" points to the tendency to exclude, and is a *psychological* dynamic that seems to reside most comfortably in the upper echelons. Of course people making their way up the ladder often lose sight of their "lower" origins. Popular discourse is full of references to "climbers" who forget or reject their former colleagues. But this phenomenon appears to be a function of the ascent itself, as if it is a natural effect of the climb. If so, then we are faced with a situation where the Law's affinity with objectivity and abstraction results in pinched organizational structures psychologically predisposed to disconnection, blindness, and abandonment.

Young lawyers often speak of their disillusionment with the practice of law. Young partners often speak of their surprise at the peculiar anticlimax that comes with partnership. Partners and other lawyers at the height of their careers often speak of a mysterious sense that, despite their nominal success, something basic is missing in their lives. In each case, the heightened expectations that the lawyers brought with them up the ladder have contributed to their disappointment. We will return to this recurring paradox of success later, but in the present context it suggests the possibility that the hierarchical imagination tends to gild the higher reaches with a false gold. Why, exactly, does the associate want to be a partner? What is it, exactly, that he or she expects to acquire, accomplish, learn, discover, or become at the mountain top?

The Age of Reason is sometimes called by another name—the Enlightenment. Isn't that the Law's promise? That if we adopt the reasoned life of objectivity, abstraction, and categorization, then enlightenment awaits us? When a forty-five year-old partner laments "Is this all there is?" isn't she suggesting she assumed something greater was in the offing? Just think how often we imagine the Wise Old Man sitting alone on the mountain peak, away from the distractions of everyday life, communing one-on-one with the wisdom of the ages. We look to the highest courts for the highest wisdom, expect leaders to have revealed answers unavailable to the masses, and even see God in the High Heavens. There is an enduring psychological pattern of associating height with heightened awareness, encompassing consciousness, clearer insight, and greater wisdom. Built into the hierarchical mind is a belief that abstraction and transcendence are the roads to enlightenment.

This belief, whatever its philosophical merit, is a prescription for disappointment because it strains against more earthly, low-level concerns of everyday life by assuming wisdom resides only at the peaks. It would be worthwhile for the Law to remember the childhood lesson that what most often is found at the top of a tree is the realization that it's a long way down.

PARTNERSHIP AND PROPERTY

In the last decade or so the legal profession has seen marked changes in the job mobility of its practitioners. Whereas not so long ago a young lawyer entering a law firm might well expect to live out his or her active career within that same firm, today many, if not most, lawyers will not retire from the firm where they begin their practice. Partners, historically "home grown" from within the ranks of associates, now are as likely to come from lateral moves. This has led to a situation where partnerships increasingly are asked to decide whether to "make partner" a person whom they don't really know on a direct, personal level. Of course resumés are circulated, and the potential partner's book of business is carefully examined, but missing is a sense of the potential partner as a person, a sense that in the past was based on years of working together in daily practice. It's like being asked to choose a spouse through mail order.

The word "partner" itself refers to sharing in a whole, being a part of a whole. But what is the "whole" the partner shares in and becomes part of? One way of answering this question is from a business perspective; a partner shares in the assets and liabilities of the partnership. But even this is not as clear as it once was. In today's legal profession there are equity partners, limited partners, and a host of hybrids. These partnership tiers are intended to differentiate between the kinds of "sharing" in which various partners are allowed to partake. (The use of tiers indicates that we still are operating under the sway of mental habits associated with hierarchy. Only within a mind-set built on hierarchical thinking could a phrase like "Up or Out" find currency as a way of describing a person's career options.) But there are other perspectives on what it means to be a partner.

The legal concept of partnership is a thirteenth-century creation. "Partner" is derived from "parcener," a related word that referred to a joint heir or co-heir. These old meanings led to using "partner" to refer to a spouse, and eventually "partner" came to be used in other contexts implying joint endeavors—one can have a dance partner or a tennis partner. The word even slipped into nautical usage as "partners," which referred to a framework of timbers round a hole in a ship's deck used to support a mast, capstan, or something of the sort. In each of these usages, we see a recurring theme of support, mutual dependence, and joint effort to achieve a communal goal. To be partners meant to stand united, to be tied to one another even beyond death as joint heirs to a common history.

And yet people had been joining together for centuries before the thirteenth-century legal mind conceived of partnership. What was it about this concept that was so appealing, so generative of new ways of thinking about relationships? First there is the degree to which the concept of partnership fit into the legal culture of the thirteenth century. This era in history saw an incredible expansion of the law into everyday affairs. Writing, which in no small measure was spread as a result of its use in law, was at last bringing the law to bear in ways unimagined in earlier times. Nowhere was this more true than in the documentation of property and land ownership and transfer. It was here that the idea of "parcener" or joint heirship arose. In an almost feverish attempt to bring systematic control to an area of social interaction that for countless years had progressed on the basis of symbolic transfers (the passing of a handful of dirt, a key, or other object symbolizing the *res* or thing being transferred), the medieval legal mind began to create ways of objectively identifying discrete and definable interests in things.[5] Partnership is one spin-off of this burst of legal creativity.

In some ways, the legal profession returns to these original concepts when it ignores more personal aspects of partnership and focuses instead on defining partnership in terms of property interests. Partnership as currently used in the legal profession has two primary meanings: one as a designation of status, and the other as a way of identifying the property or profit interest a person has in his or her firm. The medieval legal mind would find the latter familiar and comforting. But what I hear repeatedly from today's lawyers is a longing for partnership to mean that they really are part of something communal, something that identifies them as standing shoulder to shoulder with others in a joint endeavor, something that means as partners they will fall heir to the traditions of their particular firm and that they will help to create a legacy for heirs yet to come.

When partnership no longer has these communal connotations, it has reverted to its original, medieval usage as a term of division ("partition" comes from the same roots). And yet there remains a deep desire for partnership to mean more than a mere designation of property interests.

The almost comical creation of multiple partnership tiers reflects the historical tension between property and person. By making multiple tiers, an organization tries to protect its property interests while paying nominal tribute to people who otherwise might have to be rejected by the organization. The problem with this approach is that it is muted by the very hierarchical mind-set that creates it. Once equity partnership is established as the brass ring, few people who aspire to it will be satisfied with limited partnership status, a status that they are apt to view as second-class citizenship. Multiple tiers work well as a way of controlling distribution of profits to equity partners, and they are useful as a means for the partnership to avoid tough personnel decisions; but as a means of engendering community, multiple tiers stink.

Without a doubt, many modern law firms believe they exist

for one purpose only—to make the maximum amount of money possible for the equity partners at the top. It is in these firms, and in firms aspiring to be like them, that problems of loyalty seem most likely to arise. Within such firms, it is becoming distressingly commonplace to value people solely on their current money-making potential with little if any attention being given to non-monetary factors—length of service, ability to teach and mentor new lawyers, involvement in bar and civic activities, and the like. The attitude instead is best summed up by a phrase I hear over and over from lawyers in therapy. Despite their hard work and sometimes many years of service, lawyers increasingly feel as if their firm's guiding attitude is "What have you done for me lately?"

The saddest and most disgraceful examples of this breakdown in loyalty occur when a lawyer gets on in years and begins to slow down a bit. I have heard numerous stories of lawyers with thirty or more years of experience being shuttled into smaller offices, having their secretaries either taken away or assigned additional duties, and effectively (if oh so subtly) being snubbed within the firm. The bottom-line says you matter only as long as you produce, that you are what you earn; to paraphrase Descartes, "I produce therefore I am." If you want a big office all you have to do is pay for it. The problem, of course, is in what we construe as "payment."

Elder lawyers are not the only ones feeling the breakdown of loyalty, not by a long shot. Many, many lawyers feel they don't have any real security with their firms, or that their firms wouldn't stand behind them in a crunch. And let's not forget there are good reasons for them to feel this way. During the economic recession of the late 1980s and early 1990s, many firms fired large numbers of associates and partners alike simply because of an unwillingness to share the sacrifices necessary to maintain the existing job base. To add insult to injury, many of these firms refused to acknowledge that these cuts were economically driven and instead claimed they were firings based on "merit." Others hid behind faddish economic talk about the need to "get lean and mean." "Getting fired" went from "getting laid-off" to "reduction in work force" to "downsizing" to "rightsizing" to "decruiting" as such firms struggled to find sterile language to anesthetize the effect of their conduct. Of course anyone watching the trend knew such claims either were outright lies or that law firms had just a few years earlier hired hundreds of incompetent lawyers or had allowed incompetent partners to hang around too long for no good reason. A more accurate reading is that the *property-oriented imaginations* of these partnerships were blind to the human costs of their actions.

When loyalty erodes, paranoia takes over. With the ascendancy of economic Darwinism, fear becomes the by-product. Lawyers expend enormous amounts of energy in an ongoing attempt to cover their own asses. Worse, such an environment leads to a "me first" mentality that is more than willing to blame mistakes on whoever isn't present while rushing to take credit for success even if undeserved. Chest-beating is actually encouraged under such a regime, and ambition can become a thin veil for greed and selfishness.

The broad-based breakdown of loyalty within the legal profession reflects the property/person tension inherent in the concept of partnership. To treat an elder lawyer in a disgraceful manner without enduring the rebuke of conscience, a person must first make philosophical decisions that have far greater psychological implications. The question is whether a partner's value to the partnership is going to be measured only in stupidly economic terms. Once personal value is equated with productivity and the capacity to generate revenue, the ethical dilemma of how to relate to the elder lawyer is breached. Under this view, a partner owes no duty of loyalty to anything except enlarging the partnership's bottom-line. Personal friendships, long-standing service, managerial competence—none of these is relevant once the conversation is defined by economic terms. Things become black-or-white, asset-or-liability. "Will this act result in bringing in more revenue?" becomes the *only* relevant question that need be asked. At its extreme, this kind of reductive, simplistic thinking depreciates the notion of justice itself, as if the ageless quest for truth and fairness can be found on the pages of a ledger book.

Such a mind-set runs contrary to deeply rooted humanistic and religious themes. After all, it is precisely the ability to think of human worth in property terms that allowed slavery to flourish for centuries. Disrespect and contempt for the poor similarly depend on this kind of thinking. Over time, a personal philosophy based on economic measurement must lead to the same breakdowns evident in economic history on a larger scale: recession, depression, and collapse—all of which are primarily *psychological symptoms.* In the kind of paradox one sees often in therapeutic work, the typical reaction to these symptoms is first to deny them ("We had to let a number of people go on the basis of merit evaluations") and then to increase the very activity that led to them in the first place ("We have to grow ourselves out of this depression. If you want to keep your job you have to increase your productivity by fifty percent, and, by the way, you only get two weeks vacation from now on"). Once the legal mind opts for property over person, recession, depression, and collapse are inevitable.

The extent to which an imagination dominated by property-oriented metaphors is blind to other considerations is quite remarkable. I heard about one firm that set out to establish a long-term strategy for the partnership. Now here, I thought, was a good idea. Here was an opportunity to inspire a communal vision for the future. Goals could be set around which the troops could rally in a joint effort for mutual accomplishment. Imagine my surprise (and the plummeting morale within the firm) when the goal turned out to be making the firm one of the ten biggest in the city within five years. When I asked one of the partners of this firm why it had decided to strive to be among the ten biggest instead of the best, she looked at me with confusion. It was then I realized that in her mind the two terms were synonymous. To a property-oriented imagination, quality and quantity are one.

Drawing the distinction boldly, let us say there are two approaches to partnership. One thinks of partnership primarily in property terms. We can call this the Medieval approach. The other concentrates on the relational aspects of partnership, recognizing everyone within the firm as a "partner" only to the degree they contribute to the firm's mutual endeavors. This more humanistic view we can call the Renaissance approach. In the Medieval firm, primary attention is given to increasing productivity to enhance the bottom-line. In the Renaissance firm, concerns about job satisfaction, the relationship between the firm and its clients, quality of work product, and long-term viability of the firm *as a firm* are apt to be given greater consideration.

Obviously, these artificial distinctions are not necessarily exclusive. After all, both approaches are implied by the multiple meanings of the word "partner" itself. But it is striking how often the different approaches do become exclusionary. Once either approach is adopted as a dominant perspective, it colors the entire culture of a firm, a person, or a society. The task for the psychologically astute Modern partnership is to recognize these historical themes and to refuse to allow either to set up a fiefdom over the other.

INSIDE AND OUTSIDE

Another feature typifying how the legal profession is organized is the distinction between in-house lawyers who work within corporations and outside counsel who work either within law firms or as solo practitioners. Much has been written about the shift within the legal profession to having more work done in-house, and about the expanding relationship between in-house and outside lawyers, but what makes this distinction even more interesting is that the in-house lawyer of today is more apt than ever before to have come to corporate practice after spending time in a law firm or as a solo practitioner.

Notwithstanding this last fact, concealed prejudices linger between many in-house and outside counsel. Some outside counsel believe in-house lawyers are second-rate, that they "retreated" in-house because they couldn't cut it in the "real" practice of law. Some in-house counsel think of outside counsel as self-interested opportunists, necessary evils O.K. to bring in to clean up a mess but not the kind of people you want to get too comfortable hanging around. Most lawyers don't think this way, but the discriminatory attitudes are there, and are excellent examples of how deeper psychological patterns and mental habits can affect professional life in subtle, sometimes insidious ways.

As with other forms of discrimination, especially discrimination persisting among educated people, it is hard to point to clear examples. It is even harder to know for sure whether the people who perpetuate the discriminatory attitudes are aware they are doing so. In many ways, overt discrimination (racial slurs, sexual harassment, religious bigotry) is easier to address because of its clear and present danger. But discrimination among professionals and other educated people is far more subtle, often wrapped layer within layer of half-rationalized beliefs. At the same time, these subtle forms of discrimination manifest in indirect ways. (Recall Judge Learned Hand's remark that mental habits "indirectly determine our institutions.")

Sometimes, for example, discrimination against in-house counsel can be as simple as cutting them out of a case by withholding information, by not copying them on correspondence, by not returning phone calls, or by sending over filings for review only when it is too late to make any changes. Sometimes it takes the form of treating in-house counsel like a secretary whose main function is to provide deponents and other potential witnesses when instructed to do so. And sometimes the discrimination can be detected only in the bemused eye of outside counsel as he or she listens to in-house counsel's thoughts, usually unsolicited, about trial strategy or such. The subliminal message here seems to be something like "Go ahead, I know you must enjoy playing lawyer, but of course *I* am the expert here." It's as if outside counsel has forgotten that in-house counsel is a colleague, that both are charged with the responsibility of counseling the same client.

Outside counsel's assumption of the role of expert, and the "I'm a lawyer and you're really a corporate executive" attitude, are not just matters of professional arrogance. That would be bad enough. But such discriminatory attitudes go deeper than that and, as with other forms of discrimination, can say much about the psychological assumptions and insecurities of the bigot.

The in-house/outside split echoes a tendency in modern society to polarize things into an "inside/outside" opposition. "Inside" is taken to be the world of subjectivity. It is thought to be full of emotion, misperceptions, delusions, vague feelings, unrealistic sympathy, repressed conflicts, and so on. "Outside," on the other hand, is taken as the world of objective, verifiable truth. Inside is beyond rational understanding and control—we might "share" feelings but we cannot define them. The outside world follows natural law, and, in theory at least, can be understood, explained, even controlled.

The discriminatory attitudes between in-house and outside counsel reflect the broader, cultural discrimination between "outside" and "inside." With this idea in mind, let's look again at our examples.

"I'm a lawyer—you're a corporate executive." What outside counsel seems to be saying is that real lawyers stay "outside" non-legal corporate structures. This suggests both that outside counsel is suspicious of non-legal corporate structures, and that in the mind of outside counsel such structures are outside the

confines of the fraternal order proper. Furthermore, outside counsel is implying that there is something intrinsic to the non-legal corporate world that taints in-house counsel's legal judgment and makes him or her less lawyerly. Outside counsel's attitude seems to be "You can't be trusted because you are on the inside. You are subject to too many internal pressures and are too likely to parrot the party line. You are blinded by your allegiance to the corporation. Worse, you are beholding to the corporation and probably are more interested in protecting your job than in telling the corporation what it really needs to hear or in giving me all the facts." Very often, especially in the early going of a case involving in-house and outside counsel, these suspicions are almost palpable.

Just listen to the assumptions hidden in outside counsel's derogation! You can only be a lawyer when you are not "subject" to "internal" concerns. Clear vision requires independence (the fantasy of the "independent counsel") and the avoidance of heart-felt allegiance. Once subjugated to internal considerations, we necessarily lose our courage and become preoccupied with self-preservation. We become unwilling to face things squarely. Clients, who don't want to hear the truth anyway, must rely on the objectivity and courage of outside counsel for the truth.

"Go ahead and tell me your ideas, but of course I'm the expert here." This notion of being expert implies that outside counsel is superior by virtue of his or her knowledge and experience. Outside counsel becomes the worldly counterpart to the naïve, sheltered in-house counsel whose experience is limited to in-housework. We have seen this kind of patronizing discrimination for years: "Look, honey, I know you mean well, but just take care of things at home and leave the business to me."

One irony in all of this is that relatively few outside counsel have ever worked "inside" while an increasing number of in-house lawyers have worked "outside." Outside counsel's derogatory ideas about in-house counsel simply don't comport with the facts. They must therefore be understood in terms of their *fictional dimensions:* fictions because they are not based on the kind of objective, verifiable evidence in which outside counsel ostensibly takes such pride; fictions because they are made up; fictions because they seem to persist on their own despite objective evidence to the contrary; fictions because they fall victim to ideational unconsciousness and perpetuate the very kind of subjective fantasies outside counsel deride the most.

Outside counsel's lack of respect for in-house counsel also reflects outside counsel's own uncertainty about his or her own internal affairs. It is no secret that many lawyers, and the Law itself for that matter, have trouble with what are often termed the more emotional, subjective aspects of life. We have noted that the number one psychological complaint among lawyers is a feeling of inadequacy and inferiority in interpersonal relationships. From this viewpoint, outside counsel's discriminatory attitudes toward in-house counsel can be seen as driven by outside counsel's mistrust of his or her own feelings, beliefs, and emotions. *When outside counsel berates in-house counsel's allegiance to corporate concerns, we also are seeing a deep-seated pessimism that close relationships cannot be trusted and must lead inevitably to disillusionment and betrayal.*

I emphasize discrimination directed toward in-house counsel because I have experienced it to be more pervasive than that flowing from in-house counsel toward outside counsel. (The only similar discriminatory pattern based on job classification that is more pervasive is the broadly held belief among practicing lawyers that law professors are "too wimpy" to make it in the real world of everyday practice. Perhaps there is more to this reaction than first meets the eye. Perhaps it is in part a reaction based on a repressed antipathy toward legal training. Or perhaps it is an example of how one group of inductees can come to think of themselves as the "core group" while ostracizing other inductees who move beyond this self-defined "core.") But in-house counsel are not immune to the inside/outside mind-set, and often display subtle forms of discrimination all their own. One often hears in-house counsel speak of their outside counterparts as if they are interlopers insensitive to the inner needs of the corporation. I have heard in-house counsel refer to outside counsel as "parasites" and "bloodsuckers." Just as the "outside" perspective is suspicious of the "inside's" purported subjectivity, so the "inside" is suspicious of the "outside's" purported coldness, lack of sympathy with corporate concerns, and amoral tendencies.

As long as this mutual suspicion continues, discrimination will beget discrimination and the relationship between in-house and outside counsel will be based on mutually perpetuated paranoia. Disputes will continue to erupt over billings, petty one-up-manship will continue to supplant meaningful communication, and both in-house and outside counsel will continue to waste valuable time looking for ways in which the other is trying to take advantage.

One way out of this impasse is to reject the false polarization between inside and outside. After all, which is which is largely a matter of perspective. A different view might emphasize the common bonds between in-house and outside counsel. Each brings its own unique blend of experience and training to the shared obligation of representing the client. In fact, perhaps in-house and outside counsel could rely on the client as a bridge by which to leave behind their respective discriminations. There is much to be gained. The client receives a united partnership of representation. Outside counsel gains a much needed sense of community and a new respect for internal affairs. And in-house counsel invigorates its perspective by reaching beyond the confines of the *corpus*. As usual, the surest way to eradicate discrimination is to pay more attention to the ties that bind than the differences that separate.

IS TIME MONEY?

I started practicing law at about the same time that personal computers were becoming affordable. The firm where I worked decided to provide P.C.'s to all of its lawyers and to teach us how to use them. The idea was to increase productivity by allowing lawyers to revise their own documents instead of having a secretary do it, and to shorten the overall time it took to produce a new document. Both goals were fulfilled, sort of. Lawyers started revising their own documents, and the P.C. made it possible to change and reprint a document in a fraction of the time it took before. But something else also happened. Where once a document might go through three or four drafts before it was finished, it became commonplace to see eight, nine, ten drafts or more, all in about the same amount of time it had taken to do three drafts before. And yet the quality of the writing did not noticeably improve; the tenth draft was no better than the third, and we weren't winning or losing more cases or motions than before. The tenth draft was different, yes, but not better, and it soon became apparent that the process of going from start to finish was taking about the same amount of time as before. One thing *had* changed, though—the drafting process had become more harried and anxious, in part because of the proliferation of drafts. Curious.

Similar phenomena followed the appearance of overnight mail and fax machines. I lost count of how many times I faxed or sent a letter by overnight express even though there was no real reason for the rush. One putative reason was that acting quickly gave the appearance of efficiency and responsiveness and therefore made for good client relations. But again a fly appeared in the ointment. Responding quickly became habitual, and at times began to rival responding wisely. Not consciously of course, but then habitual action seldom is fully conscious.

A related story:

A young man who recently had lost his job at a large law firm came to me complaining of a lack of direction in his life. Early in our first talk together, he told me that although he was only twenty-six he had a long and impressive resumé proving he was a go-getter. He had even brought a copy of his resumé with him, and tendered it to me with obvious pride.

"How would you describe your life without referring to your resumé?" I asked, setting it aside without a glance.

"What do you mean?" he asked. He had noticed with obvious irritation my failure to review his resumé. "My resumé is my life, it lists all the things I've done." He was clearly more than a little upset that I hadn't looked at it.

"For the sake of discussion, what if in twenty years you haven't added anything to your resumé? What would that mean to you?"

"It would mean I was a failure," he said softly. A swallow caught in his throat, and dry tears filled the corners of his eyes.

A failure. As if the worth of a life could be judged by the length of a resumé.

III

What are we to make of such stories? Sounding the anti-technology alarm misses the point. Word processors, automated factories, even fax machines, are wonderful inventions (well, maybe not fax machines). And in any event our tools cannot be held responsible for our problems. No, the problem is deeper than the cult of technology. As the young man's resumé story graphically depicts, our anxieties in this area implicate how we imagine time, productivity, and their relation to personal identity.

In my therapy practice I have found that difficulties often arise when we are not precise in how we imagine things. Images and fantasies, like people, have their own identities and don't like being forced into inappropriate relationships or confused with other individuals. If imagination is taken as guide, then mixing metaphors must be seen as a psychological mistake, not just a grammatical one. So we might ask whether time is suffering from imprecise imagination. Have we forced time into being something it doesn't want to be?

Time has been pressed into the service of a guiding metaphor of modern consciousness — productivity. Productivity, in its usual meaning of producing tangible things that can be counted or otherwise objectively measured, is at the heart of modern conceptions about time and, I might add, personal identity. This correlation between time and productivity is probably one reason we find ourselves talking so much about technology when we talk about time. But what happens when productivity subsumes time?

The enslavement of time to productivity is summed up in the cliché "Time is money." Time = Productivity = Money. Given enough time we could all be rich. But if time is money then money is time and bank statements are the truest historical accounts. Under this view, putting money in the bank is like storing time, even though we all know you can't take it with you. Here we get an insight into the problem of the young man with his resumé. Note how he was imagining his identity in terms of linear advance and accumulation of credits, much in the same manner as building a financial portfolio. At the first sign of detour or doubling back he went into a panic. For him such moves were steps backwards, debits, demotions, erasures of past accomplishments, and were akin to death itself. If it couldn't be tallied on a resumé it didn't count, a fact made obvious by his inability to talk about himself as a friend, a son, a lover. In a not uncommon paradox, what he took as the problem—a *lack* of direction in his life—was actually already unconsciously present in excessive form. In many ways he was suffering from an *excess* of direction. His life was pinned to a timeline with all the arrows pointing one way. When this formalized fantasy of time no longer matched his actual experience of life's vagaries, he quite naturally became disillusioned and afraid. But it was his hardened view of time that needed attention.

When time is subjugated to productivity then productivity becomes King. All subjects must submit to the decrees of production, and things not tied directly to increased productivity become incidental if not wasteful. Time-motion studies seek to eliminate such "wasteful" actions to a point where every movement is orchestrated to produce. From this perspective, taking time for personal interaction is irrelevant because it is not cost-efficient. Better to be rude than to take too much time.

Another side-effect of this viewpoint is the mentoring crisis within the legal profession. Experienced lawyers are unwilling to take the time necessary to mentor new lawyers into the traditions of the profession because they cannot bill such time. Is it any wonder that more than fifty percent of all lawyers say they have no mentor, no one who is interested in their careers? Mentoring doesn't have a readily identifiable product, and takes a kind of time that cannot be controlled. The bottom line? Productivity deems mentoring irrelevant, a waste of time.

Productivity enlists another unspoken tenet of modern life in its oppression of time. Progress. From productivity's perspective, progress means increased productivity. Furthermore, productivity uses progress as a moral imperative—we must progress or die. If a word processor allows us to produce more drafts in a shorter time, then *we must do so*. The drive for increased productivity becomes self-fueling, locked in the perpetual one-upmanship of supply and demand. It doesn't matter so much whether what we produce is *better*. Quantity, not quality, is productivity's guide. We don't call it Gross Domestic *Product* for nothing. From this perspective, the mere fact that we can turn out more drafts on a word processor necessarily means we have progressed beyond Mr. Remington's typewriter.

Computerized time management programs and day-minders unwittingly make things worse by insisting that time problems are "data-based," as if time is a container of fixed size waiting to be filled up with discrete bits (bytes) of scheduled events: breakfast at seven-thirty, catch the eight-fifteen train, read mail from nine to nine-thirty, a lunch meeting at twelve, an hour to "work out," dinner at seven, kiss the kids goodnight at eight forty-five, sex on Sundays at nine. When people say they would be lost without their day-minders they are telling the truth. Few things scare the modern Puritan more than the prospect of unscheduled, open-ended time. Some say idleness is the Devil's workshop.

A lawyer complained to me about his homemaker wife: "I don't get it," he said. "I asked her to stop by the dry cleaners for me today and she said she didn't have time. I mean, *what does she do all day?*" Sound familiar? In many different forms, and certainly not always spoken by men about women, such comments are common. And at their core is the confusion of time and productivity. In the business world there usually are some indicia by which to measure productivity—the company made more money this year, or sold more shoes, or whatever. But not all activity lends itself to such measurement. How to measure the time spent with a young one who requires constant attention? How to measure the time spent cleaning and cooking and maintaining—all things that in the end seem merely to return us to the *status quo*? How to measure the subtle increases in comfort and love and security that occur when a homemaker makes a house into a home? Hidden in the lawyer's question was the belief that because such activities don't produce cumulative results in the manner of the lawyer's "work product" they therefore didn't take time. There is another, more insidious implication as well. If a person or activity doesn't "produce," then questions must be raised as to their intrinsic value. Compare this with the view of Heraclitus, whom some call the father of depth psychology, that "Soul has its own principle of increase."

Every fantasy brings its own peculiar morality. The fantasy of productivity preaches that increased productivity is good and reduced productivity is bad. Long resumé = worthwhile life; short resumé = insignificant life; no resumé = no life at all. The fantasy of productivity exalts efficiency and rapid growth while describing a slowing or lack of productivity in negative terms of recession, depression, and crash. From productivity's perspective, time is always limited, always running out. To reach productivity's goals we have to get an early start. We have to push our children to achieve adult skills at increasingly young ages so as to "get a jump" on the competition (that is, Everyone Else). We have to get to work early and stay late. Career spans shrink as older people are pushed out of the workplace to make room for younger people, all with the condescending implication that older people are "used up," while younger people are "fresh" and "new" and therefore can be more productive. No matter that evidence continues to mount that working harder and longer doesn't necessarily correlate with increased productivity.

Productivity insults people when it thinks of them as interchangeable parts in the engine of production. Even the well-intentioned go astray, falling into the habit of thinking of people as "human resources" to be "managed to maximize their productive potential," as if a human life can be likened to so much coal in a mine. Caught in a fantasy that says we must produce more and faster, productivity demands we punch the clock; life lived on the pattern of the nine-to-five (or, more accurately nowadays, the eight-to-six). Do or die.

But increasingly, people are running into a kind of psychic wall. Often this happens in mid-life or later, but it can happen any time. After thirty years with a firm, a partner is asked to leave because his billings are down. After taking time off from her career to raise a family and make a home, a mother encounters the incredible fact of a legal profession actually *antagonistic* to her re-entry into the workplace. Or a forty-year-old in perfect health suddenly becomes depressed and unable to concentrate on his work. When such walls are hit, questions long dormant revive. What does it all mean? Is this all there is? Have I been doing the wrong thing all these years? I have a resumé the size of a novel but my kids treat me like a visitor from out of town. And so on. Within such rumblings is the return of time from its exile in the work camps of productivity.

Can we extricate time from the quagmire where it is interwined with productivity? Can we take time to imagine time differently? We can take a lead here from the Renaissance physician Paracelsus, who said that practice should not be based on speculative theory but theory should be derived from practice. Applying Paracelsus' admonition to time, do our theories and beliefs about time match our practical experiences of time? And what about time's enduring relationship with soul? Could soul suffer because we are forcing together the mixed metaphors of time and productivity?

The principal fantasy that binds time and productivity together is measurement. Although it is unclear nowadays whether time measures productivity or productivity measures time, in either event the role of measurement is unquestioned. *Unquestioned assumptions point to how and where we are unconscious.* The more basic, common, typical, fundamental, usual a belief or a style of consciousness is, the more we are unconsciously influenced by it. When we talk about something as being self-evident we are pointing to fantasies so hidden, so powerful, that it doesn't even make sense to say we *believe* in them. Fantasies don't need our belief.

Measurement is such a fantasy. It is extremely difficult for modern people to imagine time without measurement. Seconds, minutes, hours, days, weeks, months, years, decades . . . think of all the terms we have for dividing time and collecting it in quantified groupings (sixty seconds to the minute, etc.). The fantasy of measurement requires consistency. To measure time is to say time is essentially consistent, that this second is the same as the last one and any second yet to come. Clocks require consensus, and here is where things start to rub.

For the ancient Greeks and Romans, measured time meant daytime and was measured primarily by sundials. For the ancient Chinese, Japanese, and Koreans, measured time could be either daytime or nighttime and was measured by water and fire. Burning incense was one way these cultures had of measuring time independently of the sun, allowing a person to tell time by its scent.[6] But even the Greeks, with their passion for measurement and abstraction, could not speak of time simply in terms of measured time. For these ancient cultures, *time had quality* and was not imagined as an objective, homogeneous medium. For the ancients, time was "[n]either chaotic nor mechanically regular, [but] appeared to be the work of other minds."[7] This sense that different times had different qualities led the early Greeks to believe that certain times brought certain changes and that a particular time might favor a particular activity while being disadvantageous for another. Similarly, the early Chinese talked about nighttime in qualitative terms of sunset, dusk, after dusk, waiting for dawn, and dawn, all terms that relied on relating one *quality* of time to another.[8]

Is this not the way time actually is felt? When we say, "This has been a long week," or "Is it ten o'clock already? I feel like I just got here," or "Time flies when you're having fun," are we not pointing to this enduring sense of time having quality? Compare a twenty-minute thunderstorm from the perspective of a person watching it from their kitchen window and that of a sailor in a small boat on a big ocean. Isn't time different for those two people, and doesn't the concept of "twenty minutes" blur the qualitative distinction of the times they have experienced? Just think about how time goes faster when you are heavily involved in a project requiring sustained concentration, or when a deadline is approaching. We all know time speeds up when there is an hour's work to do and only thirty minutes left on the clock. Conversely, ask a teenager sitting in history class at three twenty-five on a Friday afternoon and he or she will tell you that the last five minutes of class before the bell can take hours—especially if the teacher hasn't called on you yet.

What is particularly important about the ancient perspective of time having quality is that it values our different experiences of time and suggests that they are possible because time itself is varied. This is in marked contrast to a scientific worldview that says any and all experiences originate in the human and are then projected onto other things. To postulate that time has quality eviscerates this humanistic arrogance and respects the possibility that time itself is qualitative, that time comes complete with a range of possibilities and preferences.

There is an old and continuing debate among philosophers and scientists about the nature of time and our relationship to it. The details of this debate are not as important for our purposes as is the existence of the debate itself, because it is striking that as a culture we have more or less accepted a given way of imagining time while people who devote their entire lives to such matters cannot so agree. Isn't there room in our imaginations for more than one fantasy of time? What would happen if we were to *complement* our usual view of homogeneous time with a deeper imagination that recognizes and respects time as qualitatively diverse? After all, just because we can manufacture clocks that agree doesn't mean time is essentially the same now and always.

Imagined mechanically, "time" is a connecting concept that attempts to hold together different experiences under a single rubric, a single style of consciousness. As we have seen, this style of consciousness in turn gives rise to certain results, many of which have become troublesome and disorienting. But what if instead of "time" we imagined "times"? That is, what if we paid more attention to time *as actually manifested in this or that particular experience* than as a "unifying" (but actually devitalizing and dissociating) abstraction? Another way of saying this is that our conceptions of time are not contemporaneous with our experience of time. Must we imagine life as a rocket in the sky—accelerating, climbing, peaking, decelerating, falling, burning out, crashing? Surely the bell curve is one of the great atrocities perpetrated on imagination.

I want to be careful here not to confuse the idea of time having quality with the trite and insulting modern cliché of "quality time," a catch-phrase excuse for neglect. "Quality time" implies that if we can't spend *actual* time with friends and family, much less with the world and with ourselves, then we can distill significance and value into just a little time (thereby freeing up more time for being "productive"). And yet we all know in our hearts that a weekend of zoos and ball games cannot replace the day-in and day-out grace of time lived together. Soul requires real time, time that has room for pauses, and silence, and inactivity; time lingering like a summer afternoon, stretching lazily into evening without a care in the world, time to putter about, a day gone amidst odd jobs and piddly things.

Time allows things to happen when they want to happen. A day at the zoo can be qualitative or not, depending not so much on our personal whims or good intentions as on whether time favors that particular activity. Here again is the ancient idea that time has propensity and provides a charged context in which some things can happen favorably while others cannot. If so, then we must be more attentive to our actions, more cognizant of whether they are temporally appropriate. Acting at the wrong time can lead to unpleasant consequences, like the bad taste of an untimely kiss.

CHAPTER FOUR
THE LITIGIOUS MIND

BY NOW, certain patterns are beginning to emerge. Again and again we get the sense that the Law has a mind of its own, its own preferences and peculiarities. As within any genre of imagination, we start to, if not expect certain things, at least not to be surprised by them. Like Sam Spade with a bottle in the bottom drawer.

Images tend to cluster around other images with which they have an affinity. Some colors seem to go together, some people seem to gravitate to one another, some symptoms seem to coalesce in complexes and syndromes. Within the realm of imagination certain images seem to like one another's company, and where one appears we might expect to find others of its kith and kin. And yet, despite these familiar assemblies we also know imagination to be indirect, ever-changing, and capable of creating new images. Imagination is what it is, and yet more than it seems.

One of the most powerful images in the Law is *adversity*. Ours is an adversarial system of justice, predicated on the belief that if two sides each do their best to win a case then the best case will win most of the time. Even taking into account a wide disparity in legal talent, or that one party might have a greater ability to pay for better representation, the modern mind nonetheless believes justice is forged in the crucible of adversity.

During the Middle Ages, it was not uncommon to have litigants subjected to trial by ordeal. Perhaps this meant having a litigant hold glowing hot irons in his bare hands, or throwing him into water to see if he would float or not. Whatever the particular ordeal, the underlying belief was that God would reveal the truth through the outcome of the ordeal.

Closely associated with this belief in divine intervention was the belief that winning was the best and final proof of rightness. In fact, the distinction between "right" and "wrong" as abstract principles was unknown to litigants during these early days. Rather, given the broad acceptance of oracles, omens, and a more general acceptance that God would put things right, the archaic mind tended to see winning as an end in itself, a kind of divine vindication. For the medieval litigant, winning *was* everything.

Given this background, what to make of the modern lawyer's preoccupation with winning at all costs? The usual "cause" given for this attitude is that competition and economic pressures have driven lawyers to be hyper-aggressive and consumed with winning. But there is more to it than that. When a modern litigator sends a knowingly burdensome discovery request with the intention of "wearing down" the other side in a "litigation war," he or she is mimicking conduct from a time when might literally made right. When the legal profession places winning over altruistic ideals, it is returning to its barbaric roots.

The return of barbarism in the context of winner-take-all litigation endangers the very ends the legal mind seeks to ensure. If winning supplants idealism, then anarchy, the Law's Great Enemy, must follow as all sides do whatever is necessary to win. The argument that the quest for winning is proper as long as it is carried out "within the rules" is simply another way of saying the End is justified by the Means. In a system fixated on winning, moral and ethical considerations become *ex post facto* commentaries by whoever is left standing.

Litigation's fixation on winning is psychologically corrosive. Just listen to a group of lawyers talking about themselves, with pride mind you, as "hired guns." Or read legal periodicals that tell cute anecdotes under the rubric of "War Stories." What does such talk mean? That lawyers think being a hired gun is an appropriate metaphor for one's professional life? That war is funny? Can there be any doubt that such attitudes eat away at the lawyer, eroding the banks of morality?

THE LITIGIOUS MIND

There are deep connections between an adversarial system of justice and the idea of litigation. We could say simply that litigation is the process by which the work of the adversarial system is carried out, a kind of practical counterpart. But adversity and litigation are more than co-workers; they are kindred spirits.

The words "adversity" and "litigation" themselves declare a natural affinity. "Adversity" comes from roots meaning "opposing, hostile," while "litigate" means "to carry on strife." What is significant about these old meanings is that they provide the first clues that the adversarial system, in the form of litigation, is not really meant to resolve conflict. Rather, the psychology of litigation suggests that *litigation is dedicated to carrying on strife, not resolving it.*

This point is essential for understanding the hidden forces driving litigation. The litigious mind is devoted to strife because strife gives life to litigation. Litigation lives only so long as strife is maintained. Resolution of conflict means death to litigation. In a Darwinian struggle to survive, litigation must keep strife alive to preserve and perpetuate itself. It's a matter of litigation protecting its own self-interest.

Every litigator knows that litigation can take on a life of its own, get out of hand, make things worse, create new problems and enflame new grounds of conflict. And all of this regardless of how closely the litigation is monitored or how open to compromise the parties seem to be. Like a story determined by its ending, litigation must be recognized as a psychological force in its own right.

In practical terms, this means that litigation must find ways, systemic if possible, to establish itself. One way litigation does this is through setting up a complex system of rules and procedures designed, in practice if not intent, to perpetuate litigation. Litigators are especially prone to being swept up in these processes and procedures because the legal mind is trained to think in terms of procedure. Confronted with a tome of civil procedure, the legal mind doesn't think "You've got to be kidding, nobody needs this many rules!" Instead, it's love at first sight. Everything is an intellectual puzzle to the legal mind, and it immerses itself in figuring out the myriad procedures. No matter that the procedures are themselves neither coherent nor rational. All of this suits litigation to a tee, because once the lawyer gets lost in a forest of procedures the litigation can charge ahead under its own head, unencumbered by the lawyer's interference or intervention.

A perfect example of all of this is how the litigious mind reads the rules governing a particular conflict. The most important thing the litigious mind wants to know is what the rules will *allow* and how they can be used against the other side: how can they be stretched for advantage, not what are they intended to accomplish. It is symptomatic of this mind-set that when courts passed rules allowing judges to sanction lawyers who filed frivolous lawsuits, these very rules quickly deteriorated into a cottage industry of motions for sanctions. Surveys of lawyers suggest that fights over the application of these rules, which were intended to curb misconduct, have become one of the most common breeding grounds of incivility and abuse. Not surprisingly, a central concern among courts that have suggested the adoption of professional codes of conduct as an answer to incivility is the recognized danger that such codes might provide still new battlegrounds in the litigation war.

The litigious mind's dedication to carrying on strife also is reflected in the business of litigation. Law firm billing structures, for example, reward controversy and discourage settlement. The longer the lawyer sits at the deposition table, the more questions propounded, the more motions filed, the more baiting letters sent, the longer the meter continues to run. One "successful" litigator I know has a button in his office that reads, "Why Settle?" Indeed. But we must be careful not to mistake these mercenary manifestations for the underlying fantasy of litigation that sustains them. As long as the litigious mind dominates legal practice, lawyers will unconsciously enact the psychological desires of litigation. Practice will perpetuate conflict.

LITIGATION AND THE FEAR OF THE UNKNOWN

The litigious mind is especially concerned about the unknown. Just as doctors now routinely order a battery of tests to detect a one-in-a-million illness, litigators similarly exhaust every avenue of inquiry in large part because they are terrified of missing something. Neither the doctor nor the lawyer has any idea what that something might be, which is exactly what makes the whole process of looking for it so anxious and un-nerving. When you read twenty pages of deposition transcript devoted to questions about where the deponent went to school, you are reading a testament to the litigious mind's fear of the unknown.

It isn't really clear why litigation is so hung up over the un-known. What's the worst that could happen? Maybe a smoking gun turns up that destroys a carefully constructed case. So what? If the case was constructed on false premises then presumably it *should* be destroyed. No, it isn't that the litigious mind is afraid it will turn up something that will make it lose, but that it might turn up something that will make it *unnecessary*. Remember that in its heart of hearts, litigation itself doesn't care as much about winning as about perpetuating the conflict; for litigation, resolu-tion of conflict is the only defeat.

Given its voracious tendencies, litigation must be closely monitored. But there is a danger to watch out for in trying to monitor litigation. We saw how the litigious mind turned a rule permitting sanctions against lawyers into a tactical weapon. So too, the litigious mind will turn all efforts to control it into fights. It will resist restraints on its essential contentiousness and look for ways to free itself up. An example of this is when a cli-ent, who usually is more interested in settling things than the litigator, begins to question the litigator's legal maneuverings. But the litigator doesn't like being second-guessed, especially by a lay person, and so assumes the client is hiding something, is weak-willed or naïve, or maybe isn't willing or able to pay the fees necessary to "properly litigate" the matter. These are re-sponses of the litigious mind. When the litigious mind senses a threat to the litigation, it will use any and all means at its dis-posal, and will sacrifice whatever or whomever is necessary (including the client and the lawyer), to sustain the litigation. Although lawyers and clients are technically necessary for the litigation to continue, if either stands in the way of the litigation it has ways of dealing with them.

ARE WE AFRAID TO MEDIATE?

A while back I read an interview with a group of litigators about the topic of alternative dispute resolution ("ADR") and mediation as possible alternatives or adjuncts to litigation. A little later I read a similar interview with a group of business executives. The two interviews could not have been more at odds. To a person, the litigators eschewed the ideas of ADR and mediation, arguing that they were as expensive and time-consuming as litigation, casting aspersions on the talent and fairness of arbitrators, and generally assuming a paternalistic "maybe someday" (but not in this lifetime) attitude toward the whole concept of mediation. The executives thought differently, said ADR and mediation made a lot of sense, had great potential, and should be pursued with vigor. The litigators acknowledged that many clients asked about ADR, but concluded that it was not "being put into practice." Meanwhile, one executive wondered what it would take to make ADR "part of the environment rather than the exception."

The steadfast and collective rejection of mediation by the litigators raises questions about the ability of an adversarial, litigation-based system to comprehend and appreciate the possibility of alternative approaches to resolving conflict. It seemed as if the litigators didn't *want* mediation to be a good idea, that it was being shot on the ground without being given a chance to fly. The impression left was childish—"litigation is our game and we're not going to play, or allow, any others."

It isn't enough to chalk up the litigators' reluctance to bureaucratic intransigence or genteel foot-dragging. A more likely alternative is that the litigators' resistance was based on fear. The litigious mind sees the possibility of alternative dispute resolution or mediation as a direct threat to the litigation process itself. In particular, concepts like mediation and compromise are antithetical to a system defined by adversity. "Compromise is not Victory," whispers litigation. "Mediation is for sissies," adds adversity.

At the same time the litigators were demeaning mediation, they also were repeating the comforting and reassuring idea that clients want litigators to be "gladiators," "tough fighters," and "tough, mean SOBs." Maybe. But isn't it also possible the litigious mind tells itself what it wants to hear? Psychotherapy teaches that the shortcomings and evils we see in others often live most profoundly within ourselves.

Mediating conflicts is different from litigating them. "Mediate" means "to be in the middle," a far cry from litigation's desire to carry on strife. Mediation evokes images of stepping into a fight to break it up, not of choosing sides and joining the fray. Litigation wants a good fight and justifies its fighting with the claim that whoever wins was meant to win. Mediation wants to stop the fighting, to work out a resolution.

When one of the executives wondered whether mediation could become "part of the environment," he put the question precisely. The adversarial environment is, by definition, a hostile one. Certainly there are times when litigation is necessary, just as there are times when war cannot be avoided. But have we created an environment of hostility that by its very nature cannot entertain a real desire for peace?

What if litigators were to turn a more aggressive eye toward the rigid and atrophied ideas that dominate litigation itself? Why not explore settlement first, instead of putting it off until later when the other side has weakened, or the meter has been allowed to run a little longer? And what about the knee-jerk reaction that if the other side wants it then we must be against it? Or that the standard by which to measure a position is the "red-face test"? Or the essentially barbaric idea that justice emerges only through adversity? Or, God forbid, litigation's First Commandment that litigators must "zealously represent" their clients? Is that what we want? A profession of zealots? The legal profession cannot hope to mediate for others until *it* becomes more psychologically receptive to meditation. The profession can start by mediating the Law's assumptions about the nature and necessity of conflict.

WHY DO WE SUE?

Having looked at the litigator, what of the litigant? What to do about the national pastime of suing one another? Why, increasingly, is "sue the bastards" our first response to a deal-gone-south, a slip-and-fall, or a broken promise? What is the lure in litigation?

So much has been written about the litigation explosion that it has become a cliché. Various reasons for the drastic increase in litigation beginning in the 1970s have been propounded: Lawyers became a class of private "attorneys general" advocating newly recognized personal "rights" previously denied hearing; lawyers became more mercenary in their marketing practices, especially in the area of personal injury, and thereby encouraged reluctant litigants to sue in larger numbers; or lawyers simply became more greedy and realized the money was in suing, dragging out the conflict, and then settling just before trial. The problem with such theories is whom they leave out. Most civil litigation requires a private individual who decides to sue. Theories blaming the litigation explosion on lawyers are passive-aggressive responses. They raise the anger and anxiety associated with the litigation explosion and then pass all responsibility for it to lawyers. But such theories fail to touch what it means to live in a litigious society where *individuals* increasingly turn to the courts to solve their problems. In fact, I wonder if the adolescent nature of such theories ("Everything sucks and it's your fault!") doesn't have something to do with the apparent inability of increasingly large numbers of individuals to handle their own affairs. It's as if adolescent narcissism, with its immature and fragile self-image, is preventing us from dealing as equals with our fellow citizens.

Why do clients sue? One short answer is that they encounter a problem they are convinced must be addressed but, for one reason or another, don't feel capable of handling themselves. If either part of this equation is missing, if the problem is one the client can accept without need of further resolution or is one the client feels capable of dealing with personally, then a lawsuit will not arise. If we take this as a working hypothesis, then an increase in litigation means: 1) clients are less willing to accept problems; 2) clients feel less capable of handling their problems directly; or 3) both.

In the first instance, the client decides he or she simply is not going to take it any more. Lines must be drawn, positions taken, face saved. In every conflict that cannot be ignored or written off, something important and unspoken is at stake. Perhaps it is a moral or ethical principle, or a deep-seated prejudice, or a political ideology, or a psychological complex that hardens the problem into conflict. *It is never just a matter of money.* The increase in litigation then suggests a rise of militant moralism, an intolerance that transforms alternative views into opposing ones. Unsure of our own beliefs, we seek to have them validated by a higher court.

Once we have an intolerable problem, how to resolve it? Here, the decision to turn to an expert reflects the modern belief that there is an expert for every problem. On a deeper level, this relinquishing of lay competence to ever-burgeoning strata of specialists may be at the heart of the passive-aggressive tendencies mentioned earlier. Once we accept that only experts can speak with authority, then our own voices grow weak and timid. Agents become principals. We see this move everywhere: Only psychologists can understand our souls, only doctors can treat our bodies, only lawyers can solve our disputes. The handing over of personal responsibility and authority to experts can be fragmenting and depersonalizing, leading to a sense of non-responsibility and helplessness. Worse, when the backlash from such passivity comes, it tends to be excessive and misdirected. In a society where only experts can resolve disputes, vigilantism is almost sure to follow.

So how to counsel a client hell-bent on suing? First, determine what really is at stake. If the client insists it is money, then look for issues of value. If the client says it is to stop an intolerable business practice, then inquire into the source of the intolerance: What is being protected and what is being defended against? Is that single rogue agent who stole a client list really a threat to the corporate body, or does he seem larger than life because he represents something fearful or repulsive to the corporate mentality? Do the personalities of the potential adversaries have anything to do with the looming sense of unavoidable conflict? What is the fight really about? Although it is difficult for lawyers to see past their legal training, it is important to remember that people don't sue just to enforce their "legal rights." Always, more is at issue.

Second, ask whether the client is turning to the legal process for resolution or absolution. Again, what does the client really want? Litigation has a way of sterilizing disputes by replacing everyday reality with abstractions. In the context of litigation, a longtime supplier becomes simply "the defendant," while damning words one party would never speak to another and that can never be erased become memorialized in "a complaint." It is often just this sterility a client is seeking from the legal process. Once a matter is "turned over to the lawyers" it is "out of my hands."

Litigation performs a great disservice to the client by giving the false impression that the client can pursue the conflict while avoiding the messiness of personal involvement. (Here again we see the subtle influences of objectivity and abstraction drawing us away from involvement.) But anyone who has ever been through a lawsuit knows this is not the case. Lawyers must work against the allure of this false impression by reminding the client that litigation will *increase* his or her involvement and responsibility, not lessen it. Absolution has a price.

THE LAWYER AS SYMBOL

Ask any lawyer about his or her primary professional obligation and you are apt to be told something like "to represent my client to the best of my ability." The concept of representation is so basic to the legal mind that it feels like it has always been there, as if it is necessary.

But if we turn to religion and philosophy, we find great and enduring debates over the very idea of representation. Wars have been fought over the meaning of representation; great religious codicils influencing entire cultures have been written to define it; and disagreements over its ultimate significance have divided philosophy at least since Plato and Aristotle parted ways. There are issues of great importance for the legal mind hidden amidst this history.

In religion and philosophy, if we say something "represents" something else we are talking about symbolism; the bull is a symbol of strength, the dove a symbol of peace, etc. But, as usual in religion and philosophy, disagreements soon arise over what we mean. For example, the symbolic transfer of meaning is at the center of a centuries-old religious debate over whether religious objects are *only* symbolic representations of a higher power, or whether such objects themselves have intrinsic religious value. If the former, then smashing a statue of the Virgin Mary means only that I have destroyed a lifeless object. If the latter, then destroying the statue means that I have violated a divine presence. This might sound like esoteric semantics, but it has powerfully influenced the history of religion and the modern western mind.

To a large extent, our modern culture has opted to believe that a symbol's primary importance is its representative power and that the symbol itself lacks inherent power. For most of us, breaking a religious statue might evoke a sympathetic or nostalgic response, but we aren't apt to see God laying broken at our feet. And so in literary criticism we interpret every word as a symbol for a meaning once-removed (although some still insist the text is inviolate); in art criticism images, shapes, and colors are routinely assumed to stand for something else; and in psychology our dreams, memories, and reflections are interpreted *ad nauseam* for their latent (i.e., symbolic) meanings. The relevant issue in all of this for the lawyer is what happens to the thing that is being taken as a symbol (this statue of the Virgin Mary, this particular painting of a bull, that old man in my dreams last night). When taken as only symbols, as only representations, these things lose their particularity and are discarded in favor of the things they supposedly represent. When a psychologist translates a specific dream image of a sixty-ish woman in a flowered dress into a symbolic representation of the Great Mother or Nature, what has happened to the woman in the flowered dress? We no longer need her. Why? Because we have replaced her with a transcendent idea assumed to have greater significance.

This style of symbolic thinking riddles everyday life with practical implications. The spouse who fights to retain his or her identity in the lee of a more "powerful" or "important" professional spouse is feeling the reductive threat of the symbolic mind. There are careerists who, after defining themselves primarily as representatives of a profession for thirty years, look up to realize they no longer know who *they* are. There is the actor who struggles against being typecast by that one role played a decade earlier. But the symbolic mind does not like being confused by notions of personal integrity or change; it likes things nice and simple; for it (and I must admit for me, too) Sean Connery will always be James Bond.

Symbolic reductionism also affects our social discourse. One of the most striking aspects of modern life is that there are no little things. An unwanted kiss becomes an instance of gender discrimination or worse; a presidential haircut becomes a symbol of distant and aristocratic government; trying to save a beautiful animal isn't good enough its own right and must be recast in more grandiose terms of protecting the ecosystem. Everything is an example of something bigger, weightier. There are no small slights—every debate escalates to fighting words. How easily the symbolic mind translates individual experiences into abstractions and how quickly it entraps us in lifeless systems and stupid distinctions.

And the individual lawyer? He or she disappears into the symbolic significance of being "a lawyer." Just look at the stereotypes, typecasting, knee-jerk assumptions, and blind bigotry that lawyers endure. Even worse, look at how lawyers perpetuate the very symbolism that drains them. *People believe they have a right to see the individual lawyer as representative of all lawyers because lawyers define themselves as representatives.* It is lawyers who insist they can represent viewpoints with which they disagree, and clients whom they find reprehensible, without such representation having anything to do with the lawyer's personal integrity. It is lawyers who claim to speak symbolically, to only be representing another, sometimes invisible authority.

Although this understanding of a lawyer's role has practical benefits and might even be necessary, you see how it leaves the individual lawyer open to being reduced to his or her symbolic function. (Think how often associates in law firms talk about feeling "fungible.") When this happens, the individual lawyer is lost just like the woman in the dream is lost when we translate her into a symbolic meaning. The voice we hear only *seems* to be that of the lawyer, while deep down we know it is not the lawyer's voice but the client's. The positions so aggressively advanced, the arguments so dutifully made, the displays of indignation and outrage, the choked-voice show of emotion—we know none of these are truly *of* the lawyer but are charades and affectations assumed on behalf of another. We know lawyers are only representing clients. We know lawyers are only representations, that they are not *real.*

And the individual lawyer? Gone. Lost in the translation.

III

The view of the lawyer as a symbol surfaces very clearly in an image that has long coexisted with the lawyer. In the vernacular, a lawyer is a mouthpiece, an adjunct to the client that does all the talking while the client sits silently on the sidelines pulling the strings. Have a question? "Ask my lawyer," says the client.

One definition of "mouthpiece" is "a part, as of an instrument, that goes in the mouth or to which the mouth is applied." The lawyer as mouthpiece is thus transformed into an instrument that produces sounds according to the client's wishes. (What lawyer has not had the feeling of being "played" by a client?) Coupled with this notion is the idea that the mouthpiece is a part that can be replaced or discarded more or less at will—if one doesn't work, get another one. This version of the mouthpiece image lends itself to cliché: a crowded courtroom a-murmur as the client leans over, hand cupped to shield his own mouth, to whisper into the ear of the mouthpiece who then straightens before the microphone (one mouthpiece to another), and transmits a translation of the client's story. Everyone wonders "What did the client really say?" Meanwhile, despite his or her active participation, and even despite the appearance of being a central figure in the drama, the mouthpiece vanishes.

What effect does all of this have on the lawyer? Nobody likes being thought of as a part, or instrument, or a symbol. (Think how irritating it is when someone says to you "I know what you mean" and then proceeds to make clear they have no idea what you mean.) Treating a person as fungible is demeaning and leaves him or her feeling used and a-part. It also sets up a situation where the person has two choices: give up and allow himself or herself to be emptied and poured into another container, or fight back in an attempt to salvage his or her own identity. One recalls the curious desperation in the lawyer's cry: "I am not a potted plant!"

The effort to retain personal and imaginal integrity can take many forms, some more passive, some more aggressive. In the context of litigation, this effort can appear in the guise of hardball tactics and sudden outbursts of uncontrolled rage. When a litigator inexplicably flies off the handle, one possibility is that we are witnessing the joining of two overpowering currents: the natural antagonism of the litigious mind and the rebellion of the soul against the forces of representational thinking—forces that ignore the essential value of the individual. It would be nice if we could moderate litigation's mean streak, but it is hard to find fault with a soul fighting for its own integrity. Litigation, like politics, can make for strange bedfellows.

INTERREGNUM

WE PAUSE TO CONSIDER where we have been and what we are doing.

Part One has attempted to present some of the Law's fundamental psychological tendencies. To do this, we have been imagining the Law as having an integrity independent from, or at least not reducible to, its human practitioners. This is in keeping with a long and honored tradition within psychology of imagining human endeavors as having a transpersonal core, as if there is something going on that is more than human, something perhaps even divine.

One reason this style of imagination is difficult is because we live in the age of "human potential." It is one of the guiding myths of our age that the human is primary, the most noble and divine of all creatures. According to this myth, the human race rules the earth by means of its rational capabilities; only humans are conscious; and only humans can be said to have souls. If we need proof to support this myth we need only look to our alleged superiority over other animals, a superiority evidenced by our dominion and control, terms not incidentally of special importance to the Law.

This myth posits a pre-Copernican psychology with the human at the center of a universe enamored with our talents and abilities. Unfortunately, this myth suffers from the same fundamental problem as pre-Copernican astronomy—it doesn't fit all the facts. Left out of this prevailing myth is an enormous range of experiences pointing to other, less heroic, and less anthropomorphic conclusions. Foremost among these discarded elements is a recognition, appreciation, and respect for the autonomy of imagination. Like the early astronomers who were under orders to make things fit into officially accepted, if wrong, cosmologies, we find ourselves forced to sustain the myth of humanism by finding ways to ignore, subsume, or at least explain away actual experiences of the soul's power.

These intellectual charades are not easy to sustain. Although we continue to applaud the emperor's new clothes, every person knows the kind of experiences we mean when we talk of the soul's sometimes irrepressible influences. Perhaps we fall in love, become depressed, go a little crazy, are racked by insecurity, or gripped by the memory of loss. Whatever the particulars, in each instance we have a deep and distinct feeling that what is happening is beyond us, that we are not fully in control, not fully responsible. Just recall the last time you fell in love. Remember? Remember how you tried to work, to pretend nothing had happened? But your mind was inflamed with thoughts of the beloved—Where is he right now, what is she doing, whom is he with, does she love me, will it last, have I lost her . . . I can't sleep, I can't eat, I feel so confused, I think maybe I have a fever. I wonder if I'm sick.

We need not be so dramatic. Dinner time is coming and you and a friend are going out to eat. "What do you feel like eating? What do you have a taste for?" Where do the answers to such questions come from? Isn't it the case that a taste *comes* to the tongue? That flavors emerge from the homogenous backdrop of hunger to give precision to your desires? Not just hungry now, but hungry for *something*.

Or you are driving down the road and a song comes to mind. Maybe a song you don't even like. It persists. You find yourself whistling it while you walk, humming it in the elevator. You can't get it out of your head, you say.

Or in the midst of a good day and for no good reason at all you suddenly feel rotten, bitchy, mean. Or you wake up after a night's sleep tired and troubled, or perhaps buoyant and supercharged. We "are in" these moods, unable to extricate ourselves regardless of our conscious preferences.

And need we mention the dreams that come and go in the night?

The life of imagination is ongoing. Certainly it is most evident when fueled by passion, desire, or grief, but it also is there in a thousand little ways, continuously influencing our daily lives despite strong-willed, humanistic denials to the contrary. The rational mind always seems to be two or three steps behind experience, trying its best to impose a semblance of order and meaning in the wake of the imagination's inherent multiplicity and mystery. But such efforts inevitably end up a patchwork of exceptions and deviations, much like what happened when early astronomers tried to make their observations fit into the old Ptolemaic theory.

The Law is only one of the soul's imaginings, and, as we have seen, has its own direction and plumbs unknowable depths. *This basis in soul gives the Law its instinctual quality and numinous authority*, and there is a sense in which lawyers serve the Law as holy men and women serve their Gods.

The Law as Macrocosm is like a world unto itself. And yet at the same time it also exists within the soul's limitless sea, a powerful current, yes, but only one of many.

The image of a deep-sea current is an apt one, rising and falling, now submerged beyond reach, now tickling the surface with tell-tale ripples, giving the appearance of general direction while unexpectedly turning back on itself in self-contained eddies, sometimes resembling a road willing to carry explorers with God's Speed, other times spinning downward out of control as if reaching for the earth's own center, sometimes languid and rolling as a midsummer river, other times charging and wild, clashing with opposing currents in titanic battles whose aftermaths cloud distant cities halfway around the globe.

The Law doesn't like such talk. Metaphors, images, feelings, emotions—these things exist beyond the realm of rational control and order. Although it might be too much to proclaim them as the Law's enemies, it is fair to say that the Law prefers certainty to uncertainty, finality to ambiguity, knowledge to mystery. Perhaps the greatest irony of the Law is that it is its nature to go against nature, to work against soul's inherent diversity.

And that brings us to the lawyer.

You will have noted how, again and again, we have drifted from more philosophical considerations to practical examples, from statements about the Law to stories about lawyers. This is because the relationship between Macrocosm and Microcosm is one of interpenetration, indirection, and mutual support. We can't figure it all out or be sure about where one ends and the other begins. We can never be quite sure where we are in all of this, never settled about what we are talking about, never certain. One way of looking at any occupation or profession is to see it as an attempt to satisfy the deep influences at its psychological core. This places the lawyer in quite a predicament, a mortal in service to the Gods. On the one hand, the lawyer feels a compelling need (like the compulsion of love) to run with these professional currents, to be the kind of lawyer the Law expects, to stand for the Law's ideals, and to further the Law's interests. But on the other hand the lawyer is only partly a lawyer and feels from within the powerful tug of other currents, other needs. This situation exists everywhere and for everyone, but is harder on the lawyer because of the Law's demanding tendencies. And so the lawyer must champion control and order while knowing in his or her heart that things are neither controllable nor orderly.

It is to this tension between the Law's expectations and the broader life of the lawyer's soul that we now turn. The lawyer's lot, like that of us all, is to contain this tension. The lawyer's opportunity is to find ways to live *from* this tension, recognizing it as a source for wonder, creativity, and, yes, pain in his or her life. Wondrous and creative because it engages the lawyer in the soul's eternal quests; painful for the same reason.

MICROCOSM
THE LAWYER

CHAPTER FIVE
TYRANNY OF THE MIND

REPORTS from the field:

Lawyers are almost four times more likely to be depressed than the population at large.[9] Researchers in Washington and Arizona found one-third of all lawyers suffering from either clinical depression or substance abuse, both at twice the general prevalence rates for these disorders.[10] In a survey of 105 occupations, lawyers ranked first in experiencing depression.[11]

One in four lawyers experiences feelings of inadequacy and inferiority in interpersonal relationships, anxiety, social alienation and isolation, or depression, all at much higher rates than the general population.[12]

Forty-four percent of lawyers feel they don't have enough time to spend with their families, and fifty-four percent say they don't have enough time for themselves.[13]

Billable hour requirements for lawyers in law firms have almost doubled in the last fifteen years, now averaging 2000–2500 hours per year.[14]

Over fifty percent of all lawyers say they don't have a mentor who is interested in their career.[15]

In 1990, only thirty-three percent of all lawyers said they were "very satisfied" with their work, down from forty-one percent in 1984. Among male lawyers, twenty-eight percent said they were dissatisfied with their work while forty-one percent of female lawyers said they were dissatisfied—both numbers are roughly double those reported in 1984.[16]

A disproportionate number of lawyers is believed to commit

suicide, often "at an age when they would be expected to be most socially productive."[17]

More than half of all lawyers believe incivility is a significant problem within the legal profession and most say this is a marked change from past practice.[18]

Some states report that substance abuse is a factor in up to seventy-five percent of all disciplinary complaints involving lawyers.[19] Researchers in California and Oregon estimate that sixty percent of disciplinary actions against lawyers in those states involve substance abuse or emotional distress.[20] Nonetheless, current statistics show that for every ninety dollars spent on disciplinary proceedings, less than one dollar is spent to support programs designed to assist lawyers with substance abuse or other psychological problems.[21]

And listen to this summary of the literature by two leading researchers in the area:

> [P]reliminary empirical findings confirm that lawyers tend to be more suspicious and cynical than the general population. . . . [T]hey are more authoritarian, dogmatic, and aggressive. . . . Lawyers don't see the adoption of a dog-eat-dog Machiavellian world view as cynical, just realistic. (Citations omitted.)[22]

What is going on? Why are lawyers suffering so? And why are they so reluctant to seek relief even among their own colleagues?

TYRANNY OF THE MIND

Let's imagine the soul as a community. Like any community, the soul comprises a wide range of viewpoints, voices, and perspectives. Liberals, conservatives, socialists, fascists, religious fundamentalists, reformers of various stripes—you name it and they're there. Just think of the people, animals, and strange creatures that appear nightly in dreams, or that "pop into our heads" during the day. All of these inhabit the community of soul.

As in any community, there is a natural flux to the life of the polis. Sometimes one voice is more pronounced while at other times the same voice fades into the background. Different leaders with differing viewpoints vie for the allegiance of the populace. Values shift and change—all in the usual give and take of communal interactions. But occasionally something goes wrong. One voice decides it doesn't want to lead, it wants to rule. Very often this happens at a time when the community is especially vulnerable to overthrow. Perhaps it is coming out of a recent history of disruption, stagnation, or instability. Perhaps it feels things are getting out of control, or that its fundamental values are in crisis. Perhaps it has fallen under the sway of nostalgia and reminiscence for a golden past when people were nicer, the days sunnier, and change only optional. Whatever the reason, history suggests that such discontent can be a breeding ground for tyranny. The Tyrant has the answers, knows what's wrong and how to fix it. One of the Tyrant's great lures is the promise to get things back on track and moving again, all in return for the simple price of obedience and deference. All that is required is for the Tyrant to be given a free hand.

Psychologically and politically, tyranny occurs when one member of the community claims absolute control. In both spheres, the Tyrant adopts similar stratagems and blinds to shield the Tyrant from the oppressed. So, for example, the first step after assuming control is to disenfranchise the oppressed group, thereby depriving it of permissible means of opposing the oppression (emotionalism and involvement have no place in objective analysis). Second, keep the oppressed quiet under threat of force, and, if they press their independence, declare them a destabilizing influence and respond with violence (we must maintain order, people must be made to obey). Third, make light of the oppressed's inherent value and power through caricature and stereotype (artists are odd, women too emotional, young people too idealistic, non-lawyers too naïve). Fourth, harness the collective strength of the oppressed to serve the enslaving class (you'll need a lawyer for that, we mustn't allow legal technicians or lay people to handle legal problems). Lastly, quiet the rising bile of conscience felt by some members of the ruling class through sanctimonious claims that the oppressed are "better off" and likely would perish if left alone (without Law, anarchy).

If we press this image of the soul as community further, we can imagine our ideas, hopes, memories, beliefs, and mental habits as also part of this community. Our approach in Part I has been to imagine the Law as one member of a broader psychic population. But, as we have seen, although the Law casts itself in terms of democratic rhetoric ("no person is above the Law"), it does not think of *itself* as one among equals. The Law claims superiority—no person is above the Law because the Law is above all persons.

It is this claim to superior and controlling authority that gives rise to much of the lawyer's psychological distress. We are dealing here with a tyranny of the mind in which objective "rationality" has declared itself sovereign and is oppressing other voices within the lawyer's soul. Again and again, whether in studies or in therapy, there is the recurring theme that the lawyer's imaginal diversity has been restrained, restricted, and repressed. To make matters worse, this usurpation of communal authority has had help from several quarters—not least of which is psychology, which preaches "mental health" under the rhetoric of self-esteem, ego-strength, and integration. It is sometimes difficult even to recognize this form of tyranny because it doesn't proclaim its ascendancy outright but instead slowly erodes and weakens the soul's communal structure. Like a savvy autocrat, the Tyrant knows that a frontal attack is liable to rally resistance, so it works behind the scenes to fragment and disempower potential opposition before finally stepping forward, not as a conqueror but as a chance for better times. Recall the study of law students that found how impersonalized analysis gives a false sense of reassurance. Here is the Tyrant's promise made good: "I'm finally getting myself together; things are making sense; I know now how things work and what I'm supposed to do." Recall, too, the aristocratic overtones of legal education and training—lawyers are not just different, they are *better*, all by dint of their single-minded allegiance to the Tyrant's ways. That is why the struggle against this Tyrant is so difficult. We want to believe in the Tyrant, we want to trust its ability to protect and guide us, we want it to be in charge. As history suggests, the most dangerous Tyrant is the one who is so ingratiating that we let it in ourselves. Only later, when the atrocities begin, do we realize our mistake, and then it is too late.

The lawyer is not alone in this psychic oppression. Tyranny of the mind is also at work in modernity's blind belief in objective rationality as the supreme source of knowledge and understanding. But although this belief is widespread it exists in concentrated and powerful form in the lawyer. In fact, much of the lawyer's prestige, status, power, and mystery comes from the high degree to which the legal mind represents the modern worldview so clearly. As we have seen, lawyers are trained to place consummate faith in the powers of the intellect. The legal mind has decreed that only reason, logic, and objective rationality are capable of furthering the Law's overriding concerns with order, stability, and consistency. This makes sense, of course, because the sustaining fantasy of rational thought is that things are innately ordered or, at the very least, are susceptible to being ordered. (In fairness, this truncated contemporary usage of "rationality" bears little resemblance to the noble and inclusive meaning of that term for classical philosophers. One of the great tragedies of modernity, in fact, is the degree to which we have reduced rationality to a mere sliver of its former self.) Whether in Law, mathematics, philosophy, or science, the mannerisms of objective rationality remain: the exaltation of empirical evidence; the eschewing of emotional involvement; the demand for lack of contradiction; the bedrock belief in reason and logic; the craving for process, rules, and regulation; and the relentless pursuit of predictability. All of these appear with such *regularity* that we may take them as hallmarks of the analytic mind. And all of them dovetail perfectly with the Law's overriding desire for order.

But as rationality is exalted, other forms of psychological existence are oppressed, relegated to lower stations, and stripped of power and influence. The Tyrant, blinded by its ascendancy, sees nothing wrong with this. After all, these are second-class citizens we are talking about. They don't have the worldly wisdom, the technical expertise, the mature realism necessary to care for themselves. Here we see another of the Tyrant's most powerful tools at work, the power to define its subjects. The Tyrant will label anything that doesn't fit its program as unworkable, and anyone who questions the Tyrant's authority as hostile and untrustworthy. So, when the Tyrant declares the need for Order, all things not matching the Tyrant's definition of order become suspect. That is why tyranny leads to closed society. Once the Tyrant's definitions are in place, they become self-sustaining, locked in their own circularity. If something doesn't fit, it is either excluded or eradicated. The Tyrant sees only what it wants to see because it is foreclosed by its own mind-set from seeing anything else, like the conspiracy nut who sees plots everywhere.

We must remember, though, that none of this is meant to ignore or trivialize objective rationality. Obviously the Tyrant has great appeal and power that cannot be denied. Besides, a psychologically sophisticated mind must remain open to numerous perspectives, including that of the Tyrant. But, unfortunately, the Tyrant does not, perhaps cannot, return this respect and openness. Eventually, the objectively rational mind suffers the fate of all tyrants—it comes to believe in its own superiority. It is as if the rational mind *must* believe only in itself, rejecting all other claimants in a single-minded conviction to rule. Like all tyrants, it becomes a prisoner to its own belief, alone amidst its subjects. No wonder so many tyrants claim, in the end, to talk to God.

III

Tyranny of the mind appears in the legal profession under many guises. One is an obsessive careerism that relegates all other aspects of the lawyer's life to second-class status. I remember one lawyer whose wife was pregnant with their first child. During a conference call to set a deposition schedule, this lawyer said, with considerable irritation, "I'm not sure when my wife is going to give birth." That was the Tyrant talking. Priority number one was the deposition schedule. Things needed to be decided, confirming letters written, plans made—and here was this "problem" the lawyer couldn't "be sure of" interfering with nailing down the schedule.

Two things jump out here. First is the incredible fact that this lawyer was actually viewing the impending birth of his child as an irritant. A second, and more subtle, factor is the way in which he expressed his irritation. Note how the entire situation became impersonalized through abstract language. It was "his wife" who was responsible for the uncertainty and "giving birth" was the interfering event. Not only do such phrases ring with the Tyrant's preference for impersonal language, they also help sustain the tyranny by transferring responsibility for the noncomplying event ("the birth") to someone other than the lawyer. Here the Tyrant killed two birds with one stone: It divorced the lawyer from the emotive power of his baby's impending arrival while letting everyone else on the conference call know it wasn't the *lawyer's* fault that things were uncertain.

It is tempting to write this lawyer off as a heartless ass. But he was not an ogre, and I suspect he would have been shocked if he had realized what he was saying. But he *didn't* realize what he was saying. His life had been subjugated to (literally "brought under the yoke of") the Tyrant and he was unconsciously following the Tyrant's demands for regulation, certainty, and adherence to schedule. (A variation on this theme might be the woman lawyer who, in blind servitude to obsessive careerism, chooses cesarean section—named after another tyrant—as a means of "scheduling" childbirth in accord with her work demands.)

Another lawyer tells the following story of his exit from the profession. He was a young associate at a large firm and, like most lawyers, was overwhelmed with more work than he could possibly do. One day the phone rang. His grandfather was gravely ill and the immediate family was being summoned from around the country. The young lawyer dutifully boarded a plane for the trip to the family home—armed with a stuffed briefcase and a lap-top computer, hoping he could "get some work done" during the trip. Halfway through the outbound flight the lap-top crashed, losing the brief he was working on and leaving him helpless to continue. As he tells it, he flew into a rage and in the privacy of his mind found himself angrily denouncing his grandfather as being responsible for this interruption of his work schedule. It was just then that he heard himself and was horrified at what he heard. When he returned to his firm, he gave notice and subsequently left the practice of law altogether.

You see the parallels in these two stories. Again we see how the Tyrant turns a profound personal experience into an irritating interference while simultaneously shifting responsibility for the perceived interruption to another person. Luckily the young associate caught his tantrum before the plane landed. Can you imagine the scene if he hadn't?

The Tyrant is everywhere because it *must* be everywhere if it is to maintain its iron grip. I have heard partners give assignments to associates on Christmas Eve with the clear expectation that they be completed by the next day. I have seen phone calls made to lawyers on vacation to "check a point" that was already certain, the barely hidden implication being the lawyer shouldn't even *be* on vacation. I have seen lawyers work all night to complete a rush assignment only to find the next morning that the assigning partner wouldn't be in that day. And I have seen lawyers send secretaries to select and buy birthday presents for the lawyer's spouse or children (there are even "professional services" to handle this nowadays). In each instance, we see the same bludgeoning blindness, the same subjugation of the truly important to the essentially transient. But then nothing the Tyrant wants is trivial to the Tyrant. Subjects know well the dangers of not abiding the Tyrant's wish or whim.

REBELLION AND BREAKDOWN

Tyrants always attempt to limit the form and content of expression. No tyrant tolerates free speech. So too with tyranny of the mind. Art might be appreciated for decorative purposes, but it cannot be granted the respect due intellectual knowledge. Metaphorical and poetic language is O.K. for entertainment, but is inappropriate for legal discourse because of its alleged imprecision and ambiguity. Emotions might be acknowledged, but only to the degree a virus has to be acknowledged in order to find a vaccine.

It appears to be beyond the capabilities of rationality to accept contradiction, vulnerability, ambiguity, uncertainty, and imbalance as natural concomitants of psychological life. Also, rationality's cocky air of superiority (a common trait among tyrants) indicates its resistance to being only one voice among many. How odd that the very mind-set that pays lip service to equality so adamantly demands its own unquestioned superiority.

If this seems harsh or overstated, remember the symptoms enumerated at the beginning of this chapter. The primary psychological complaints among lawyers are interpersonal feelings of inadequacy and inferiority, anxiety, social alienation and isolation, and depression. The theme running through all of these symptoms is lack of involvement and interest in the larger world beyond the Law. Lawyers are being cut off from their sense of belonging to a broader community. This detachment appears variously as an inability to sustain intimate relationships, a feeling of social ostracization, destructive competitiveness, and bad manners.

Many of the symptoms plaguing lawyers can be traced to rebellions of the soul against the tyranny of the mind. Once again, the analogy between what happens to the lawyer and what happens in political tyrannies is a close one. At first the tyranny is successful, perhaps even welcomed by the populace. Order is restored and the chain of command is clear. A sense of reassurance prevails, nationalism flourishes, discordant voices are silenced and all appears calm at last.

But soon pockets of discontent begin to form. Meetings are held behind closed doors. "Why can't we say what we believe?" asks one citizen. "What's wrong with open debate?" asks another. An elder member of the community, drawn reluctantly to the conclusion that the Tyrant is not as beneficent as first appeared, suggests a petition of grievances. Another, younger and less patient, says fuck the petition—force is the only thing the Tyrant will listen to. Secret plans are made. Weapons are gathered. Civil unrest and social fragmentation increase. Soon, innocent people begin to die.

Compare this to what happens within the soul of a lawyer who has fallen under control of the Tyrant. At first the Law's mandates appear to answer all comers. Order, rationality, and objective evaluation actually seem to quiet things down and the lawyer begins to have the feeling he or she is in control. People who once ignored the lawyer now seem to value his or her opinion because the lawyer is the Tyrant's representative. But soon cracks begin to form. The lawyer makes a mistake at the office and a partner thought to be a friend quickly distances himself from the lawyer, unwilling to be tainted by the mistake. At home, the lawyer's spouse complains that the lawyer has become distant and doesn't seem to care or to listen anymore. Friendly phone calls are replaced by calls for "advice" because the lawyer's detached professionalism has replaced friends with potential clients. Parties and get-togethers that once were chances for camaraderie and fun become obligatory and are seen as opportunities to "network." Civic responsibilities are undertaken, not out of conviction, but because they are "good career moves." Jokes that used to be funny suddenly are heard as personal attacks. What was thought to be indigestion turns out to be an ulcer. A close friend just the lawyer's age is felled by an attacking heart. Panic-attacks, most certainly indications of a soul in revolt, lay siege to the lawyer, taking his or her breath away. Sleepless nights deprive the lawyer of rest as the soul's dreams become more militant and threatening. And through it all the lawyer remains bewildered, unable to see what is happening, unable to fit all of this into the Plan, never thinking maybe it is the Tyrant who is responsible.

At last, the lawyer can take it no longer. Perhaps he or she seeks help from psychology, hoping the soul's namesake discipline can provide refuge. But the Tyrant has gotten there first. The lawyer is met with a litany of concepts designed to strengthen the Tyrant's reign: wholeness, unity, oneness, regularity, uniformity, symmetry, harmony, progression, continuity, development, self-actualization, ego-strength, regulation, organization, classification, and system. All of these concepts work against the diversity that could provide vigor and animation to the lawyer's psychic life. All work against the soul's communal nature by positing ego-strength, normalcy, and homogeneity as the models for psychic health. None give the lawyer what he or she needs—confidence in the integrity of the soul and the courage to demand that the Tyrant mind step down from its throne and take a seat at the table of communal discourse.

We saw in Part I that the Law believes anarchy to be the only alternative to Rule of Law. Just as fundamentalism sees any deviation from dogma as heresy, objective rationality sees anything that doesn't fit the categorical imperative as frivolous, disturbed, or even insane. We must remember that this is in keeping with the Tyrant's self-sustaining and self-protective nature. *To the objective rational mind, loss of control and authority feels like breakdown and death.* To admit its own limitations means it must acknowledge the very things it fears most: confusion, ambiguity, uncertainty, emotion, and craziness. What takes more courage than placing one's life on the line?

The Tyrant lacks this kind of courage. Instead we encounter a cowardice so typical in Tyrants, a cowardice expressed through bluster, rigidity, brittleness, and arrogance. We all have known people, maybe including ourselves, who, after going through a breakup with a lover have said "Never again." For a while we adhere to this maxim, fencing ourselves off from any involvement that might lead to intimacy. A hardness of attitude is put on like armor to protect us from the arrows of love and desire. Perhaps we lose ourselves in our work in yet another attempt to put a protective barrier around the wounded passion we feel inside. We become short-tempered, mean; people begin to shy away from us, which is exactly what we want; and all the while we keep telling ourselves with self-righteous conviction that this is how to avoid being hurt again.

But what of the sadness? The deep, lingering, dull ache felt most acutely in the wee hours of the morning when our self-exile is revealed for the tragic lie that it is? What of the anger behind the cynicism? The longing behind the shield? The emptiness behind the facade of activity and arrogance? Here is the excessive tithe required by tyranny of the mind, a regressive tax that depletes our emotional stores, leaving us paupers, needy, homeless. But here too is hope, for mythology teaches that Love is born of Need and that what Love needs most is Soul. The alternative is life in death, a soulless wandering without meaning or purpose, sex without love, acquaintance without friendship, and, in the words of Mark Twain, the sleep that does not refresh.

DEPRESSION AND THE DECLINE OF BEAUTY

Paul, a fifty-three-year-old partner at a mid-sized firm, complains of being uninterested in things in general and his job in particular. Everything just seems to be too much trouble. He can't concentrate on his work and feels like none of it matters anyway. His partners took up the slack at first, attributing Paul's distraction to the "mid-life thing," but now they are losing patience with his continued lack of productivity.

Ron made partner two years ago and has been on a steady decline ever since. Always a stickler in the past about his personal appearance, he has become a real mess. His hair is long and unkempt, and he has put on fifteen pounds in the last few months. His once neatly tailored suits are now clearly a size too small and are wrinkled and stained. The firm is at a loss about what to do, but it has gotten to the point where Ron can't be allowed out of the office, and his partners guide visiting clients the long way around just to avoid him.

Linda can't sleep. She is at work when the sun comes up and still there when it goes down. She barely eats and has begun to look pale and drawn. The quality of her work has declined markedly. Once careful and focused, her research now is often misdirected and her writing disjointed and confused. Her colleagues have told her to stay home and get some rest, but home is the last place she wants to be. There has been talk behind closed doors that if she doesn't pull herself together she's going to have to go.

These stories suggest the infinite variety of depression. Some depressed people overeat, others eat hardly at all; some can't sleep, others sleep all the time. But there are recurring themes in depression. One of the most common is a loss of interest. Anyone who has ever been depressed, which probably means everyone, knows that when you're depressed everything just seems blah. Depression's "I don't care, nothing matters" attitude makes it difficult to concentrate and therefore almost impossible to work. When we're depressed we don't want to be around anybody, and yet being by ourselves seems to deepen the depression. Try as we might to pull ourselves out of the depression by our own bootstraps, we remain incapable of enjoying the very things that once brought pleasure.

When we are depressed, we often feel sad, lonely, and lost. All of these feelings are extensions of the loss of interest that characterizes depression. "Interest" comes from the roots "*interesse*," which mean "to be among." Something "holds our interest" when it encourages our participation, when it occupies us. When we say we are "interested in someone," we mean that person is intriguing, engaging, that he or she holds forth the possibility of intimacy, the chance really to get to know someone other than ourselves and ourselves through the eyes of someone else. Interest connects us to other people, other things, other ideas. When we lose interest we feel left out, cut off, dejected and rejected, lonely.

Some researchers have suggested the possibility that the lawyer's work environment is conducive to depression.[23] This possibility becomes more likely if we take "environment" broadly to include not only our physical surroundings, but also work relationships and our attitudes about our jobs and ourselves. (Think, too, how depression itself has environmental dimensions, how when we're depressed, our surroundings become tinged with blue.)

If depression makes us lose interest in things, then we can restate the researchers' environmental observations by asking what it is about the legal environment that contributes to this loss of interest. How does the legal environment encourage detachment, isolation, abdication of community, and the loss of pleasure?

We know from other experiences that the most insidious environmental influences are the most subtle, the ones that build up over time and extract a long-term effect. After all, a factory spewing raw sewage into a public lake won't be tolerated for long. But let that same factory slowly and invisibly contaminate the air with invisible, odorless pollution and it can takes years before the devastating results are recognized. So too in the work environment, overtly obnoxious materials are seldom the problem. It's the little things that add up. For example, think how many lawyers arrive at work every day to an office with white-washed walls. Where the only warmth comes from a computer terminal humming on the desk. Where they drink their daily coffee from disposable styrofoam cups while sitting in non-descript, uncomfortable chairs that are like every other chair in every other office in the firm. Imagine how many lawyers live their days under the glare of artificial and false light, filling out time sheets that reduce the irretrievable moments of their lives to impersonal accounts, their self-worth defined by calculation, personal security forever tied to revenue produced. Sounds depressing, doesn't it?

Another example. Walk down the halls of many law firms nowadays and you will find little if any real art (reproductions of old lithographs of judges and lawyers don't count). Many offices are "well-designed" in terms of work efficiency, but there is an almost overt avoidance of beauty. What art *is* there is often, especially in remodeled offices, more modern—abstract shapes, blocks of color, sharp lines. I often get the feeling that such art was chosen more to accent an overall interior design than to serve as individual works of art valuable in their own right. Where are the vibrant colors of a fall maple? The subtle blues of a seascape? The enigmatic and involving eyes of portraiture? The point here is not to get into a debate over personal taste in art but to emphasize that our work spaces must be aesthetically *interesting*. Lawyers are strong-willed, and accordingly they need powerful art capable of arresting their movement, overcoming their preoccupations, and piercing the veil of "objectivity." Workplaces must be as beautiful as they are efficient; they must feed the soul's hunger for beauty if they are to provide spaces capable of holding our interest and giving us pleasure. Lawyers tell me repeatedly that they feel like their lives are dull and humdrum—all grey suits and muted ties. It's as if they are suffering from sensory deprivation, or, more precisely, aesthetic deprivation, an absence of beauty that leaves them uninterested and uninteresting. *The subtle withdrawal of beauty from the legal work environment contributes to the elevated levels of depression felt by lawyers.*

Enlarging our view of "environment," what about the many

work-centered relationships that go on during daily practice? We saw earlier how the Law prefers hierarchies (partners-associates-support staff), and we hinted as well at how hierarchies can be internalized to the point where they can distance us from ourselves. In the average law firm work environment, those lower on the chart constantly are trying to put their "best face" forward while those higher up abjure becoming involved with the underlings. Among the sub-groups themselves, individual members become increasingly isolated as competition replaces collegiality in the drive for personal success. In short, hierarchical and caste-oriented forms of law firm organization often exacerbate detachment, isolation, and a withdrawal from communal participation in favor of self-interest—the harbingers of depression. The current managerial fad of Total Quality Management, a phrase to placate the Tyrant if ever there was one, tries to finesse this point by saying we should treat our co-workers as "customers." But this merely perpetuates the subtle Me-Them divisions we are trying to avoid.

No amount of beauty or community will help to alleviate the drag of depression unless lawyers become more attuned to appreciating how important these things are. But legal education and training often seem contrary, even antagonistic, to such appreciation. Lawyers must be objective, rational, cool. And above all they must not let their emotions get in their way. Is this why the legal environment eschews beauty and community? Because they necessarily entail emotional involvement at close quarters? This *systematic avoidance of involvement* may in fact be at the heart of the lawyer's dilemma.

SUICIDE

Symptoms are always saying things, and yet they are notoriously hard for us to understand. One reason symptoms elude clear understanding is that they are not intellectual statements abiding by the rules of rational discourse. Symptoms say what they mean, yes, but in imaginative forms more akin to art, poetry, and literature. To understand symptoms, therefore, we best approach them with an eye of appreciation and an attitude of respect.

The hardest perspective to maintain in psychotherapy is one of respect for the symptom. It's especially difficult when the symptoms are so evidently destructive. Depression, obsession, anxiety—the symptoms of these and many other pathologies hurt. They tear down and oppress other viewpoints, other voices. But nothing seems more destructive, more final, than suicide.

Suicide and depression are closely linked. Both are a kind of dying. In depression this dying is metaphorical, showing up as listlessness, apathy, and general malaise. In suicide, this metaphorical dimension is what dies first. Everything becomes literal. Depression turns to despair, loneliness to alienation, and death comes to mean that the body must literally die.

III

Bob came to therapy on the edge of emotional and physical collapse. We weren't long into our first session when he became fidgety and said, with what seemed the last ounce of self-control he could muster, "There's just no way out." He told me his practice had become too much for him, and that he felt like all he was able to do anymore was "put out fires." He said he no longer had any sense of actually *being a lawyer,* which to him meant helping people avoid or find ways out of difficult spots. I asked him what he wanted to do and again he said he just wanted out.

"So," I said, "why don't you quit? You could transfer your cases to other lawyers and quit."

"I can't," he replied, and then proceeded to tell me in great detail why this simply wasn't a reasonable alternative. In his telling, every conceivable factor—from family expectations to professional ethics—weighed against his getting out of the practice. Finally he fell silent, and then, after a long pause, said quietly, "Sometimes at night I think the only thing that makes sense is suicide."

There it was. So complete was Bob's intellectual prison that the soul was playing its last card. Not only had the night-thought of suicide appeared, it had taken a particularly deadly form within Bob's imagination by seeming to make sense. What do we make of this "reasonableness"? It actually seemed as if the rational mind was supporting Bob's suicidal thoughts by creating the illusion that they were sensible. The amassing of evidence, the closing of every other door until only the "logical" conclusion remained, *the ability to think of suicide in impersonal terms*—these are all characteristics of an objective, abstract, tached mind-set. Perhaps the Tyrant had decided that if it couldn't have Bob then nobody else would either.

I asked Bob to imagine sitting and talking five years down the road. I asked him to imagine that his life was the way he wanted it to be, that everything had sorted itself out. I asked him to describe what he saw. He leaned back, closed his eyes for a few minutes, and then said, "I've got a small, part-time practice. Two days a week I work in a shelter for the homeless." Another moment passed and then he said, "I've started painting again, and I spend a lot of time with my family and friends."

Notice Bob didn't say he was dead. In the realm of his imagination the suicidal ideation had disappeared in its literal form. And yet something *had* died, namely the tyranny of mind that had given rise to the suicidal thoughts to begin with. In the depths of his imagination Bob realized there *was* a "way out" short of physical self-destruction. On reflection, I wondered if Bob's comment that suicide "made sense" was a sign of his mind recognizing its own need to relinquish control. Maybe the Tyrant wanted to step down and was trying to figure out a "rational" way to do so. When it couldn't think its way out of the box it had put itself in, it started to reach for ideas that under any other circumstance it would never have considered. In its desire to break free of the limitations its own tyranny, the Tyrant had deluded itself into thinking of suicide as a rational alternative, a conscious, considered choice.

But in Bob's fantasies of the future the Tyrant had found a way to relinquish control and was happily living and thriving as one member in a community of other interests and activities. No longer driven to be completely in charge, the Tyrant now worked "part-time." No longer itself homeless, the Tyrant now was able to help others without a home. And instead of being trapped with "no way out," Bob, in his dreams, was out and about, spending time with family and friends and giving outward expression to the soul's aesthetic sensibilities through painting.

III

The great danger of suicide lies in its literalism, not its imagination. It is this literalism that can make suicide especially deadly when it arises in the context of the rational mind, because the rational mind is already predisposed to literalism. (Research suggests that among people who attempt suicide, lawyers, who are trained to be literal, are particularly adept at carrying it out with fatal results.[24])

The therapeutic task, then, is to open the channel between the rational mind obsessed with literalism and the imaginative truth at the heart of suicidal ideation. Remember how Bob came to the conclusion that suicide made sense? I have seen this dynamic repeatedly—it is as if the suicide ideation knows what the person's sustaining fantasy is and how to co-opt that fantasy to support the suicidal ideation. In Bob's case, he believed in "making sense"; his suicidal thoughts picked up on and mirrored this belief. I also have noted another correlation. When I asked Bob to imagine the future, his fantasy was one of being reconnected to a larger sense of community. People who depend almost exclusively on literal, rational modalities to shape their understanding of the world, and who are enduring suicidal thoughts, frequently relate similar future fantasies. Often they are doing community service of some kind, and often this service relates to serving disadvantaged groups—serving food in a soup line, working with inner city schools, etc. Such fantasies raise the possibility that, contrary to views of suicide as cowardly or escapist, suicidal thoughts might be performing a metaphorical community service of their own, trying to reconnect the person to those parts of the soul that have become outcast and downtrodden, perhaps even revealing the soul's desperate desire to *re-enter* and serve communal life, not leave it.

As with other pathologies, the missing ingredient at the heart of suicidal ideation is a fundamental respect for the broader life of imagination. Suicide's literalizing darkness strangles the imagination's vitality and versatility. One cannot help but wonder if suicide's call would be less prevalent and less deadly, especially among lawyers, if we nurtured the soul's imaginative capabilities with the same degree of dedication and discipline given to more analytic pursuits.

ADDICTION AS A VARIETY OF RELIGIOUS EXPERIENCE

If suicide seeks to free an obsessed mind through fantasies of death, addiction seeks to allay it through distraction. Many addicts talk about their addictions as a kind of suicide-in-progress, and psychology is fond of talking about the "abusive" and "self-destructive" aspects of addiction, sometimes imagining addicts who have freed themselves from their addictions as "survivors." Certainly addiction can lead to tragic ends, but if we hold in abeyance our desire to end addiction and instead lend it a compassionate ear, what is it saying? What is it trying to tell us? In particular, what do high levels of addiction among lawyers say about the state of the legal soul?

One way of looking at addiction is in terms of surrender. The addict has surrendered (and please note that by "surrender" I do not imply conscious or voluntary choice) his or her life to the requisites of an overpowering addictive agent. The addictive agent slowly becomes more and more a part of the addict's life until there is a transfer of authority. The agent comes to be seen as *necessary* to the addict's life, common, habitual. At its most extreme, addiction replaces the addict's life with that of the addiction—the addiction's life becomes paramount and the addict will do anything to sustain the habit even if these things are ruinous to the addict's own life. All that matters is that the addiction be kept alive, its ever increasing desires satiated. Stories of addiction are replete with countless tales of people who have given up everything, including life itself, to indulge their addictions.

Almost anything can become the object of an addiction. The more common are well known—drugs (including alcohol, tobacco, and caffeine), sex, work, power. But people also can be addicted to religion, politics, television, money, therapy—you name it. This suggests that although there might be contributing factors (genetic, physiological, etc.) making some things potentially more addictive than others, addiction rests not only in the addictive agent itself but in the relationship binding the addict to the agent. It is the *habitual dependence* on the addiction that holds the addict's life within the confines of the addiction, defining all aspects of the addict's life in terms of the addiction.

The addiction's control over the addict doesn't have to be, and often is not, conscious. If the current fad of recovery therapies teaches us anything it is that addiction is primarily an unconscious phenomenon. It isn't so much that addicts are "in denial"—an ego-based fantasy suggesting that addicts really know they are addicted but just don't want to admit it—as that they are literally unaware of the addiction *as* addiction. Because their lives have been quietly usurped by the addiction to the point where the addiction is the defining characteristic of their lives, addicts often get lost deep in the woods, unable to see the forest for the trees. Interventions of various kinds are designed to overcome this myopia, to show the addict the addiction. At their best such interventions can be a big step toward releasing the addiction's hold on the addict's life and re-ordering the de-pendent relationship at the heart of the habit. At their worst, such interventions are indulgences of the ego's heroic tenden-cies, using the addiction and the addict as foils for the bully ego's need to take charge. In the end, overcoming denial is less a heroic achievement of the will than a simple recognition of the addiction as addiction.

We noted at the start of this section that, just as there are connections between depression and suicide, there also are connections between suicide and addiction. Both addiction and suicide have the power to overcome the person's will through subterfuge and denial, and both have a peculiar relationship to death. No wonder addiction and suicide are so chastised, so feared, and so epidemic, in a culture itself addicted to ego-strength, self-control, self-actualization, and personal growth. Addiction and suicide remind us in no uncertain terms of the limi-tations of the ego's control, and both show in stark detail that the soul cannot forever be dominated by personal preference.

To the extent that addiction and suicide expose us to the ego's limitations, they perform a service of great value. If—as addiction and suicide indicate—the powers of the soul are greater than the powers of the ego, then we should beware the inevitable results of the ego's campaign to conquer the vicissitudes of the soul. Like Icarus who flew too high, an ego following inflated ideals of its own capabilities runs the risk of self-destruction. The harrowing rise in rates of addiction and suicide indicates a self-indulgent culture at odds with soul.

Whenever we start to talk about powers beyond the self we enter the grey area between psychology and religion. Not surprisingly, both addiction and suicide have strong religious undertones and in their practice reveal striking similarities to religious practice. No matter that the prevailing views of Judeo-Christian religion are steadfast in their opposition to both addiction and suicide.[25] Despite such organized denial, the fact is that descriptions of addiction and suicide are packed with religious significance.

III

Rhonda claimed to have a drinking problem. She had been to the library and the bookstores, had read up on "addictive personalities," and had concluded that her addiction was basically self-destructive behavior based on a deep-seated lack of self-esteem most likely stemming from child abuse. She had no memories of this abuse, but several of the books she had read assured her this probably was because she was "in denial." Given the degree to which Rhonda had figured things out, it was somewhat surprising she had decided to see a therapist at all. It actually seemed more like she had come to verify her self-diagnosis.

Rhonda also had deduced a therapeutic plan of action based on her diagnosis. Her reasoning ran something like this. If she was addicted to alcohol because she lacked self-esteem, then all she needed to do to get rid of her addiction was learn to be stronger, more "empowered," more in control of her life, and more self-approving. Simple, really. Just a matter of taking charge and having a "positive attitude." After explaining all of this to me, she asked, rather insistently, if I agreed with her conclusions.

I dodged her insistence as best I could and asked her to tell me about her drinking. What did she drink? Where? When? How? I wanted details. It was clear that she didn't see much point in this inquiry, but she reluctantly agreed to humor me. She told me she always drank a certain brand of gin, noting it was an expensive, upscale brand. Her favorite way to drink was alone and the process of the drinking was precisely ordered. She would come home after work, change into some comfortable clothes, mix a gin and tonic, take it to her favorite chair, put on some music, dim the lights, have a cigarette, and then sit there for hours, getting up only to mix another drink.

"What do you think about while you drink?" I asked.

"Nothing much," she said somewhat dreamily, "I just sit there and listen to music until I get drunk and then I go so sleep."

"Do you do anything other than listen to music?"

"Sometimes I try to read a little, but mostly I just sit and listen to music."

I told Rhonda this sounded a lot like meditation to me, and I asked her how she felt about these long hours of sitting, listening, and drinking.

"That's the scary part," she said. "I think I actually enjoy myself more sitting there in my chair with my G&T, listening to music, than I do all day long. I'd rather sit there than eat dinner. I guess I do it to relax."

"Do you relax?"

"Well, yes."

"Then why do you want to stop doing it?"

Her face clearly showed what she thought of that question. "Because it isn't right!" she said. "I could be working-out, or catching up on some work, or doing something productive. I can't keep coming home and sitting in a chair drinking myself to sleep every night."

Maybe the recovery movement is right and Rhonda's drinking was a sign of low self-esteem pointing to a traumatic childhood. Or maybe the brain-doctors are right and Rhonda was biologically predisposed to alcoholism and her drinking was a symptom of a physical disease. But surely something else was going on, too.

Rhonda was describing a ritual. The particularity of the setting (a certain chair, the lights just so), the accoutrements (the clothes, the music, the cigarette), the ingesting of a valued substance (expensive gin), the precise timing and ordering of these events and their repetition (Rhonda said she always did it exactly the same way), the resulting sense of relaxation and bliss that followed (the drinking was putting her "self" to sleep)—all of these are the stuff of ritual.

As the therapy progressed, Rhonda and I began to talk at length about her spiritual life. She was raised in a devoutly religious family and had strong ties to her religion earlier in life. But these ties had weakened as she grew older, and it had been years since she had thought of herself as "religious." As we talked about this occurrence, she began to sound remorseful, as if she missed this religious dimension of her life and felt more than a little guilty about it. I began to wonder if her lost spirituality had returned in more substantive form in her self-professed addiction to alcohol ("spirits"). Certainly her actions suggested a ritualized relationship with a power felt to be beyond her control.

Whatever else one might posit as the "causes" of Rhonda's drinking, it became clearer and clearer that in her case it also was pointing to her deep desire to reincorporate spiritual and religious concerns into her everyday life. Think, for example, of the Christian ritual of ingesting the body ("corpus") of Christ as an act of "communion," as a way of embodying the spirit. Is that one of the things Rhonda's addiction was trying to do? To provide a ritual space where she might embody and commune with her spirituality?

III

That addiction can have a religious dimension is of great significance for lawyers who, as we have seen, tend to forsake ethereal concerns for pragmatism and materialism. Who knows, perhaps the excessively materialistic tendencies of many lawyers (the bottom-line as the only measure of success; personal identity tied to a corner office, two secretaries, a house in the "right" neighborhood, an expensive car, etc.) are finding perverse expression in the elevated levels of substance abuse within the legal profession. After all, in substance abuse it is the substance that is being abused, just as we mistreat material things through voracious consumption, turning things into disposable goods. Perhaps we ask too much from substances and material things when we ask them to satisfy our egocentric desires and supplant the soul's deeper needs. Burdened with our unreasonable expectations, they begin to exact their own price in return—a life for a life.

Another possibility. Might the high rate of habitual dependence among lawyers indicate a *need* to be dependent? Addictions often are characterized by withdrawal from the world at large in favor of an intense relationship with the addictive agent —the alcoholic loses himself or herself in the bottle, etc. Could it be that lawyers suffer inordinately from addictions because they too are taught and expected to withdraw from contact with the larger world and to deny themselves intense relationships with that world? What are we to make of comments from addicts that their addiction is "their best friend?" And what about the deep sense of community and mutual support that characterizes many of the groups formed to help people overcome their addictions ("support groups" we call them)? Can we read addiction's apparent isolation as in fact a manifestation of intense love? A love that wants to lock the door and stay in bed together forever, a love destined to burn up under its own intensity?

WORKAHOLISM AND OTHER WORK DISORDERS

We begin with two cases in point.

A partner tells a group of associates that in his opinion the firm has a right to expect them to commit *all* of their time to the firm in return for the large salaries they are receiving. Another partner at the meeting tries to mollify this remark by asking with a jocular smile, "Oh now, you don't mean that literally do you?" "Why, yes," says the first partner.

Another lawyer is fond of telling young associates that he never saw his wife or children when he was the associates' age. He is *bragging,* mind you, not warning the associates to avoid a similar pattern of neglect.

Case One reduces work to economics—a day's work for a day's pay. Case Two reveals an obsessive mind-set that sees work as the sum total of one's existence. Each, in its own way, sustains and perpetuates destructive relationships between work and worker. Let's take a closer look.

"Workaholism" is an ugly word. It implies a compulsive drive to work at the expense of other aspects of a person's life. The workaholic, like other addicts, loses control of his or her life and becomes habitually dependent on work. The workaholic is "taken and seized," the original meaning of "occupation," as work takes all things prisoner.

Obviously, a workaholic is different from a person who works long and hard for the sheer pleasure of it. Some people might routinely work sixty hours a week simply because they love their work. To these people I offer only the gentle reminder about too much of a good thing.

But there are other people for whom that same sixty hours feels not like a labor of love but Sisyphean toil. Again and again, in individual therapy and in larger studies of the legal profession, lawyers complain that the practice of law demands too much, that they feel trapped within the profession, that firms expect them to be totally committed and to give up their whole lives to the firm. Some lawyers say the practice "wants their very souls." Throughout the profession we hear from lawyers who say the practice of law is psychologically and physically depleting them.

Many lawyers feel troubled, but they then assume it is *their* trouble, a matter of their personal psychology, so that the answer is to learn to "cope" better, or to "share their feelings," or whatever. This view misses the fact that *work* can be sick, that the pathology can be in the work, in its organizational structures and systems of management, its professional attitudes, even its physical environs (we hear nowadays of "sick buildings"). It is only natural that many lawyers, through their sympathetic talents, begin to reflect and interiorize these work disorders. The psychological mistake is to take these disorders as the worker's problem, thereby misplacing the symptom. Instead we must open ourselves to the idea that the legal profession as a whole is showing symptoms of a strained relationship with work.

We have recounted the evidence that lawyers are working at a breakneck pace. Yet despite spending more and more time on the job, increasing numbers of lawyers feel estranged from their work, at odds with it.

What are we to make of a situation where work seems to be laying increasing claim to our time and energies while our interest and satisfaction in that work plummets? Why has work— among the most natural of activities, an activity possessing instinctual necessity like love, sex, or hunger—why has work become problematic?

Case One: "**The pay is great but I hate my job.**" The dominant style of imagining work in our modern culture is economic. We work for future reward, next week's paycheck, a partnership down the road. (Even partnership has become defined increasingly in economic terms. There are income, equity, and capital partners, for example. Within such divisions of labor, partners spend enormous energy worrying about their "shares.") The lawyer's work day has become divided into economic units of billable and non-billable time. There are budgeted requirements for lawyer productivity, law firms make economic projections and predictions, hiring and firing are tied to supply and demand, and throughout everyday practice lawyers are urged to keep an eye on the bottom line. The actual work of work comes to be seen as an unnatural behavior carried out by essentially reluctant workers. Humans become resources, assets to be managed for maximum efficiency and productivity, enticed by the promise of more money, a raise in the worker's standard of living.

I have never had a lawyer in therapy complain about the money. I have had many complain that they have lost interest in their work, that it has no value, is meaningless, just people fighting over money. Often these same people feel a lack of self-worth, as if they are not appreciated, are getting no credit, no trust. But I suspect it is not only they who are being devalued, not only they who have been depreciated, but work itself. When reduced solely to economic terms—work for pay—work begins to feel enslaving, debased. And of course work falls victim to inflationary excess. Stripped of intrinsic, instinctual value, it takes more and more work to be worthwhile, more hours, less down-time.

Recently, the sluggish economy has been a boon in promoting this economically reductive view of work. Recession and the fear of depression or collapse have provided a societal excuse for working round-the-clock and have given rise to a me-first competitiveness of distorted intensity. Law firms are told they must get "lean" by getting rid of the "fat." It's as if there is no room for voluptuousness, sensuality, comfort, warmth in the economic work place. (This repressed fatness often returning as bloated procedures and hefty fees.) People unwilling to fuel the economic engine of productivity are considered "dead wood." And communal values become replaced by rampant individualism as lawyers think in terms of economic survival and of themselves as "profit-generating centers." Darwin meets Wall Street.

We must break this definitional tie between work and pay. I don't mean pay is either unimportant or evil. My point is that focusing on pay as work's essential value forecloses actual involvement and enjoyment in work by postponing its payoff till next Friday. Like reducing love to sex, reducing work to pay has direct implications for the life of the soul—gratification found not in the hands-on intimacy of work itself but in the spending only.

A remark by psychologist James Hillman is useful:

> [I]t is disastrous to separate out satisfactions, the final cause or goal of an action, from the functioning of it. Then the functioning becomes meaningless in itself and one hurries toward the

payoff. The payoff is a displacement: you defend yourself against the joy of work, letting go in it, the libidinal passion of it by high pay, more money—and, of course, it is never enough and you feel bought or obligated. That ruins work and ruins love.[26]

The "libidinal passion of it." What an extraordinary idea! Work as an irreducible act of love, as a psychic fundamental, necessary to soul.

It is common for religious orders routinely to include work as part of their daily practice and to see work as a necessary and natural aspect of spiritual devotion. Think of the Shakers, for example, for whom every daily act is one done in service to God, and who have created and crafted so many beautiful things. The secular mind misses this connection and marvels at the coincidence that so many Shakers have happened to be master craftsmen. One approach to an answer, then, if work is suffering from a diminution of value, is to question the degree to which it has become a purely secular practice. Perhaps we need to better recognize work's spiritual and soulful concerns. After all, most of us spend most of our waking moments working. Can we truly afford to spend all of that time profanely?

Case Two: **"The law is my life, and if you want to succeed at this firm it damn well better be yours too."** Here we go further into the connection between work and soul. The lawyer who brags about forsaking family for work has put into opposition two spheres of immense value to soul. Imagine, work versus family. We see this forced opposition maintained when abstract demands for efficiency and "commitment" fight against ideas like flexible time and family leave. One woman capital partner returned from maternity leave and approached her firm about a flexible time arrangement. Her firm said sure, but she would have to give up her capital partnership. "Want a family?" says this view, "Then you must spend your capital, hand over your shares."

It's as if we are allowed to share only within the confines of partnership. Some firms talk about "limited commitment" tracks to partnership. Is that a message capable of nurturing respect between work and worker? It seems to say that people dedicated to family must necessarily "lack commitment" to the practice of law. This obsessive view of work becomes monolithic—Thou shalt have no other God but me.

But something else is going on, too. Many lawyers overly invest their personal individuality in their professional identities. In the parlance of professionalism they have "become lawyers." Once this identification is made, the person will do anything to maintain the professional persona because it has *become* them, expressive of their very being. Indicators of this condition include not being able to turn it off at the end of the day, feeling lost and uncomfortable in non-work settings, and imposing professional attitudes on all aspects of life. So often I hear lawyers say they would like to step off the track, slow down a bit, maybe do something different for a while but they fear the loss of face and worry that family and friends might think less of them if they made less money, had a smaller office, or worked for a less "prestigious" firm. But would any true friend think less of us because we change jobs? Would any parent love a child less because he or she took a cut in pay?

We all know individuality cannot be comprised solely by the strong-willed, stand on your own two feet, never let them see you sweat, I don't need anybody attitudes fostered and promoted by legal education and training. We all know true individuality requires diversity and is fraught with slips and falls, silly embarrassments, stupid mistakes, larks and follies and omissions. Often it seems we come to know ourselves best through such things, as if our vulnerabilities are at least as constitutive as our strengths, our failures as essential as our successes. And yet these are the very experiences left out of a monolithic obsession with work as *the* source of personal identity.

It is tempting to avoid the halting, start-and-stop, go-back-and-pick-up-something-left-behind process of becoming an individual by assuming the cloak of a profession. The substitution of professional persona for personal individuality can go on for years; some lawyers never get past it. But usually there comes a time when the persona slips. A strange and unfamiliar face appears in the morning mirror. It is the face behind the mask, and its unfamiliarity is a good gauge of how far we have fallen from ourselves.

No individual's life can be sustained by role playing, and certainly not by playing only one role. Obsession with work imposes just this limitation, creating an artificial environment in which the lawyer must always be "on." Yes, there is comfort in knowing one's lines, knowing where one is supposed to stand

and what one is supposed to do, but no one can endure the incessant demand to "stay in character." Typecasting might sustain an acting career, but it cannot express the range of our natural talents.

Unfortunately, this obsessive role-playing is encouraged both by legal education and by the bottom-line mentality we discussed earlier. Whether it is the archetypal law professor telling students they must leave law school "thinking like a lawyer" or a law firm structure equating a lawyer's worth with box-office appeal ("This lawyer really draws the clients, what a 'star'"), the troubling message being sent is that to "make it" lawyers must give up their private lives and adopt their professional persona. This message is reinforced by society's tendency to identify a professional with his or her profession to a degree far beyond other jobs or occupations. Ironically, one of the most painful aspects of lawyer-bashing is precisely how it deprives a lawyer of his or her own individuality, turning individual into stereotype, person into symbol.

An obsessed mind cannot see beyond its obsession, and this is true whether the obsession appears in an individual, a law firm, or the profession at large. "Of course I work seventy hours a week. Everyone else puts in these kind of hours, it's part of the job." Or, "The law is a jealous mistress." Or, "If you want to make it in this profession you have to be willing to sacrifice home and family." How similar this closed-shop mentality is to other settings where obsession becomes the defining characteristic of a group. Within a community of addicts, for example, addiction is the price of membership and the non-addicted often are viewed with mistrust if not downright disdain. When work becomes addictive it does what all addictions do—it separates and isolates the addict from the non-addicted world. Complaints and entreaties of spouses and friends are dismissed because they "don't know what it is like." Personal interests and avocations fall by the wayside because they don't contribute to sustaining the addiction. The lawyer's personality grows weaker, racked by the addiction's overwhelming power. At its worst, work addiction replaces the lawyer's friends and family with fellow addicts, and the workplace, like today's crack house and yesterday's opium den, becomes the lawyer's only world.

Once again, the big loser in all of this is the work itself. Work cannot alone define us. When we ask work to provide us with an identity we ask too much, overworking work's natural limits and capabilities. Work becomes stressed, there is too much pressure on it, and it responds in the only way left to it by becoming more rigid, reinforcing itself with increased bureaucracy in an attempt to strengthen its own interiority. Work suffers when its own virtues and desires are replaced with those of the obsession's egotistical demands.

We estrange ourselves from work by asking it to satisfy our needs instead of engaging it for its own noble ends. I am convinced that work wants to be done well, that quality of work is important not only to satisfy the demands of clients or our own need for "feedback" but because work is a natural activity of the soul. The soul takes pleasure in the careful crafting, the aesthetic dimensions of work well done. How would work change if we looked at it as an artist might, judging it not only by how efficiently it is done or by its practical result but also by its beauty? By imagining work as an Other demanding respect and appreciation in its own right, we might at once release ourselves from the artificial constraints of professionalism and release work from the bondage of egocentric obsession. No lawyer is only a lawyer and no work assignment has only utilitarian ends.

So, how to accomplish the work of re-valuing work? How might the workers of the legal world unite to cast off the chains now constricting work and the ways we imagine work? One way of showing work that we value it is to offer it the fullest range of our own natural talents. Technical ability and competence are not enough to satisfy work. Work deserves the best we have, all of us, all of the soul's imaginative and creative capabilities. We must practice law as a musician practices music or an artist practices art. More is required than reluctant, begrudging toil. In a peculiar way, the lawyers' lament that legal practice wants their soul might be pointing to a way out of this impasse. When they say this, they assume a defensive, protective posture, as if the law wants to gobble them up, chewing out their juices and then spitting them away. *But what if we were to imagine the Law's demands as its own quest for soul, as a desire for intimacy and involvement and a fuller place at the table of soul's community?* I cannot shake the sense that our current ways of imagining work are leaving the law and legal practice lonely, desperately lonely. Like so many lawyers, the work of the law also wants to break free, to be more than is currently allowed. It, too, wants to entertain new ideas and perspectives, make new friends, sail toward new horizons, and deepen its sense of history and purpose.

We don't necessarily need to make big changes. Sweeping altruism or grand ideas of systemic reform do little to touch the soul's most basic needs. Instead we must concentrate on how we do the little things. Attention, care, respect—these are things of substance and matter for soul. Perhaps this means straying beyond our job descriptions to explore our work's frontiers, or freeing responsibility from its moralistic heaviness by seeing it in terms of active responsiveness to our world. Perhaps it means avoiding the pitfalls of specialization that can further restrict our sense of what it is to be a lawyer. Perhaps it means blurring organizational lines so we might become more familiar with our fellow workers, relating as comrades instead of competitors. Or perhaps it means flowers in our offices, not only to brighten our spirits but to adorn the workplace itself.

The work of work is soul-work. If we can rekindle this fragile sense of everyday involvement, would our work then need to be so symptomatic? Work is not just an economic reality or a road to personal satisfaction—it also is a psychological reality that provides daily opportunity for care of the soul.

CHAPTER SIX
LAWYERS IN LOVE

LAWYERS SUFFER inordinately from the defining symptom of our Age—loneliness.

Research surveys refer to this deep-seated loneliness in more scientific terms as intrapersonal feelings of inadequacy and inferiority, social alienation, or isolation. One hears reference to "free-floating anxiety." Whatever we call it, we all know what it means to be lonely, and lawyers know better than most.

Sometimes, we say that we are lonely when we lack relations with other people, places, or things that matter to us. This loneliness is like an unfillable hunger, gnawing at us from within, growling for relief. In its grasp we can become prone to excessive acquisition as we try to satiate its longing. We might try to fill up on people, heading out the door to look for action at a bar, shopping mall, gym, or back at work (the latter being an especially attractive alternative for lawyers). Or we might try to load up on experiences and things, taking wildly expensive vacations, collecting techno-toys, or going to lengths to be current—the latest movies already seen, the latest books already read. But none of these tactics touches the hollow core of our loneliness, none quiets the pangs of its insatiability.

Other times the loneliness is more introverted, as if we are unable to get close even to ourselves. Like old Descartes, lying alone in his bed, staring at the ceiling, driven into himself by doubt. Only I am real, he concluded with mock certainty. But for him this was a *deduction*, not an affirmation. As if our individual being is at best what is left over after we have destroyed everything else. Individuality like a cockroach after the Bomb.

Loneliness is the soul's most prevalent societal and individual *pathos* (suffering), and is reflected in countless symptoms associated with the dominant ideas of our age. Bulimic consumerism, with its binging hunger, is a pathology of loneliness. So, too, psychology's obsessive quest for personal growth and relatedness. So, too, the spread of gangs and the burgeoning of single-issue support groups (survivors of this or that, addicts of all stripes, yuppie salons, etc.), both phenomena fueled by loneliness. So, too, our cultural fascination with and vicarious dependence on "personalities" like movie stars or athletes.

But in a curious turnabout, being lonely puts us in the best possible position to sense the actual collective loneliness of our Age. Alone in a crowd because these other bodies lack substance; the sun bright but cold; food sealed in safety-wrapped sterility, all light and clear and no calories (i.e., incapable of providing heat, useless as wet matches). The very pervasiveness of loneliness makes one wonder if perhaps it is the last greatest proof of our commonality. Perhaps Descartes was on to something after all; in a contentious era devoted to dichotomies, maybe loneliness must emerge as the ground of our being. We might divide ourselves along racial, religious, ethnic, and ideological lines, but we suffer our longing as common fate. In loneliness we are similar if not the same.

THE IMPOSTOR SYNDROME

A few months after I first started practicing law, a partner in the firm met with a group of us first-year associates to talk about our new life as lawyers. I remember him talking about something he called "the impostor syndrome," and since then I have come to believe that the impostor syndrome is a widespread phenomenon especially common in the legal profession.

Syndromes are groups of symptoms that cluster around a common theme. In the impostor syndrome, this theme is an internal, secret fear that the lawyer doesn't know what he or she is doing and is apt to be found out at any moment. Once his or her incompetence is discovered the game will be up. Everyone will know the lawyer has been pulling a ruse, pretending to be secure and knowledgeable when in fact he or she has been winging it all along. Failure and, worse, ridicule will follow while other people, whom the afflicted lawyer assumes are *not* impostors, point their fingers and snicker at the impostor's audacity and intellectual nakedness.

I remember one early bout with the impostor syndrome. It was very early in my career, and I had been assigned to assist with a document production at the office of a Very Important Client. Things were going nicely when I was approached by, gulp, the client's general counsel who handed me a document and asked me whether it was covered by the attorney-client privilege.

I had heard of the attorney-client privilege before. I remembered specifically that it was covered in the Bar Review and was confident I could explain the concept. In theory, that is. But that document? Was it covered by the privilege? Damned if I knew, and I was getting ready to tell the general counsel just that when the words of the partner running the case intoned through my memory. "Don't ask any stupid questions," he had instructed, "We don't want them to think that we aren't on top of things. We have to build their confidence in us."

So I read the document again, looked the general counsel straight in the eye and calmly said the document appeared to me to fall under the privilege. Inside I was telling myself what the hell, if I was wrong we could always produce it later. He nodded his agreement (I figured he hadn't wanted to produce the document in the first place or he wouldn't have asked) and walked away satisfied. I was surprised at how easy it had been, but then a dark thought formed like a rain cloud. Maybe he had seen through my bluff. Maybe he was on the way to tell the partner in charge of the case to send a real lawyer next time. I made a note to bone up on the attorney-client privilege at the first possible moment. (As it happened, the case went away and my "advice" was never tested—I'm sure I was right, though.)

In the early years of practice I encountered the impostor syndrome often. Just about every time I got a new assignment, in fact. I felt like I *never* knew what was going on. A partner would start talking about "letters of credit" or some such thing and I would nod knowingly as if I had just that morning been talking about letters of credit with my wife over breakfast. Then I would stride out of the partner's office and immediately scurry to the library to find out what a letter of credit was. And I wasn't alone either. Behind closed doors, my friends and I confided to one another that apparently some mistake had been made; the law we had learned was not the law we were being expected to practice.

The roots of the impostor syndrome begin in law school where lawyers are taught it is better to bluff than to admit ignorance. It is fueled by expectations that lawyers should be willing and able to advocate any position, no matter how outlandish, if it is in the "client's interest." Watch almost any trial, and you will hear two lawyers telling more or less diametrically opposed stories with the utmost conviction and apparent sincerity. This is a charade, of course. Both lawyers know they are being excessive and one-sided. Both know they are overstating their own case and being overly critical of the other side's case (note that in this context it makes sense to talk about two different cases within the same case). In fact, not only do they *know* they're doing it, they're *doing it on purpose*. This is, after all, what they have been schooled, trained, expected, and paid to do. They are *supposed* to do this. It is almost unthinkable in the current legal climate for a lawyer to acknowledge the other side's strengths, never mind admitting weaknesses on one's own side, and this stubborn fear keeps lawyers locked in confident opposition.

At what cost? Certainly the impostor syndrome contributes to already high legal fees by perpetuating face-saving battles, encouraging "cover-your-ass" inefficiency, and leaving lawyers to constantly reinvent the wheel because they are unwilling to ask for help from more knowledgeable people. Far worse is the internal toll the syndrome takes on the lawyer. At first the lawyer merely feels inadequate and dishonest. But the next step is cynicism. The lawyer decides everyone else is faking it too, and begins to relate with people on the assumption that everyone is lying and posturing. Needless to say, this wreaks havoc on the lawyer's relationships.

The legal mind finds many ways to combat the insecurity wrought by the impostor syndrome. Specializing is a favored response. Everyone knows how comforting it is to believe we know what we are talking about. On the other hand, every lawyer who has worked with experts knows how reluctant they are to stray beyond their field, how they will go to absurd lengths to maintain an already established position, how ruthless they can be in attacking alternative views, and how easily, when challenged, expert confidence transforms into arrogance. Take these natural weaknesses of specialization and add the lawyer's proclivities for self-protection, and the impostor syndrome can all but stop the honest exchange of ideas.

As with other professional attitudes, the lawyer's daily bouts with the impostor syndrome don't get turned off with the office lights. The syndrome persists in the lawyer's guarded demeanor. Like a fugitive on the run, the lawyer watches every face for the look of sudden recognition, a look signaling the lawyer that it is time to go.

LOVE AND THE SINGLE LAWYER

So here is the lawyer, feeling inferior and inadequate in interpersonal relationships but driven by education and training to exude an attitude of confidence. He or she looks at the world, including other people, through objective eyes, seeing them as objects of study—and potential troublemakers. A self-styled warrior, the lawyer interprets all real-life experiences as potential sources for adversity and conflict. Like the gunfighter, the lawyer must always be on guard because he or she doesn't know where the danger might come from; life is lived with one's back against the wall. It is against his or her professional grain to be receptive to other people's ideas or viewpoints because they are necessarily seen in argumentative form, just as the lawyer is unable to speak without sounding like he or she is in court. With these kinds of mental habits and professional practices dominating the lawyer's life, is there any wonder that lawyers find it difficult to enter and sustain interpersonal relationships?

Intimacy means, among other things, being seen for what we are by someone who is so close to us that we cannot hide our blemishes. Intimacy is based on small, almost imperceptible perceptions garnered from everyday life jointly lived; my wife knows how I do little things, like making a sandwich or brushing my teeth or holding her hand while watching television. Intimacy might include sharing great secrets, but it need not; and even when it does, such sharing is built upon the sediment of the commonplace. The breadth and depth of these deposits, their insurmountable historicity, contribute to their strength and beauty. So too, massive upheavals in intimacy seldom occur unpresaged by smaller seismic disturbances. When I hear one spouse complain about how the other folds towels or takes ice out of a tray, I begin to fear for their marriage.

If we are most ourselves in our eccentricities, we show these oddities most clearly in seemingly trivial acts. "Trivial" referred originally to a place where three crossroads meet, not a bad image for the confluent view of individuality we have been talking about. Similarly, one of Freud's more intriguing insights about dreams was how an apparently insignificant detail in a dream could be powerfully important, a psychic fulcrum capable of moving the entire dream. It is curious that lawyers, who live in a world of incredible minutiae—intricate procedures, arcane rules, tiny distinguishing facts—can be so bad at appreciating the trivial and mundane. It's as if they can only think "big" thoughts or address "critical" issues. And yet love and intimacy depend on little things. Perhaps it's just a matter of the lawyer's abstraction taking him or her too far away from what is going on. Perhaps it is the latent aristocracy we have seen embedded in the Law's self-image—like a President feeling out of place in a check-out line. Or perhaps the legal mind at some level realizes how important these little things are, how much they say about the lawyer as an individual, and how impossible it is to keep all of these little things under control. Remember the scene in *The Great Escape* when one of the POW's, disguised as a regular citizen, is about to get on a bus that will take him to freedom? The Gestapo is there checking papers. The prisoner's papers are forgeries, but after a tense moment they pass inspection. He has his foot on the step when the Gestapo agent says, in English, "Have a good trip," and *without thinking* the POW replies, "Thank you." For want of a nail . . .

This feeling of living undercover and of fearing exposure through a slip of the tongue strengthens the impostor syndrome and elicits from it a straightforward reply—keep the bad stuff hidden, don't let on who you really are, keep people where you can see them, don't stay put for long, lie when necessary. This is not so unlike how many people have come to think about relationships nowadays. "I've been hurt before and now it's hard for me to get close," we say. "I keep my defenses up until I know I can trust a person. Maybe once I know them better and that they really like me, I can let down my shield." But how to determine trustworthiness without dependence? How to know if the bridge will hold without putting some weight on it? How to know if someone else likes me when the "me" I show them is a manipulated version of myself? How to be intimate when I fear myself to be a deception? You see the problem, and it is a problem at work tenfold in the life of the lawyer. After all, the average person comes by their caution through experience; the lawyer's caution is compounded through education, training, and social and professional expectation.

In many ways "becoming a lawyer" means remaining single. By single I mean "one only" in the sense of alone, apart, uniform. This kind of single has nothing to do with marital status, and indeed many lawyers who are most single are married. I am talking about the lawyer's habitual stance as Loner: the solitary champion who stands alone against the crowd; the self-made success who makes it to the top through individual intiative, hard work, and tough-mindedness; the lone wolf wrongly shunned by an ignorant society and forced to make it alone on the outskirts of civilization; the monkish lawyer in his or her office late at night, away from worldly distractions, researching and pondering as if all answers must arise first as individual revelations. In so many ways every lawyer is a sole practitioner. They are taught to avoid involvement through objectivity, living primarily as observers who, even when they do get involved, tend to do so only on the basis of prior observation and consideration (translation: the legal mind instinctively fears spontaneity). They are taught to avoid honest, open, and free-wheeling conversation through a fear of the word (like the old war posters proclaiming "loose lips sink ships"), to boast and crow in an attempt to overcome the anxiety of the impostor syndrome, and to hide their weaknesses from fear of attack. Over and over again, lawyers—married, single, involved, or uninvolved—tell me they feel like there is a wall between them and other people. And I'm not just talking about love affairs either. This same distance shows up throughout the lawyer's relationships with coworkers, friends, family, and society at large.

The very repetition of this complaint makes me wonder if it isn't a natural concomitant to the psychological patterns we have been outlining. For example, one way of recasting the lawyer's love infirmities is to see them in the context of the ancient alleged antithesis between Love and Reason. This is a huge topic, of course, and beyond our scope here, but it is worth noting a recurring, even dominant, theme in the western tradition

that decrees love akin to madness. Early Greek poets and philosophers recognized Love (Eros) as a supremely influential de-
ity. Among all the gods, Eros alone possessed the power to drive
both god and mortal to distraction. Already, at the beginnings of
rational philosophy, an essential conflict is postulated between
Reason (as rational, controllable, and moderate) and Love (as
irrational, uncontrollable, and excessive). Plato called love a
"divine madness," and Plotinus later would refer to it as a "deli-
cious trouble." Here, too, arises the antique opposition between
Mind's lofty aspirations and Body's sordid baseness. The Judeo-
Christian tradition continued this spirit/flesh opposition by
teaching that the greatest love is the transcendent love of God,
thereby devaluing earthly, mundane, mortal love. Romantic,
possessory love of the kind associated with Eros was to be avoided,
even feared, and was defiled as demonic temptation. The best
love, the purest love, says this tradition, is not of this world.

This alleged antithesis between love and reason persists to
this day. It reappears in the lawyer's belief that objectivity is
threatened by involvement and that rationality is superior to
imagination. Mainstream psychology, itself riddled with repres-
sions in this regard, continues to encourage a paranoid attitude
toward love either by embracing Freud's libidinal theory (which
while having the benefit of recognizing love's possessory power
nevertheless considers love a disruptive influence in the life of
the controlling Ego), or by reducing love to irresistible hormonal
influences in need of moderation through education or medical
intervention.

Whether one follows the philosophical traditions that identify love with madness, or the religious traditions that seek to
control love through ministerial mandate, it is easy to see how
the Law might become suspicious and afraid of love and its affairs. These are, after all, the great intellectual rivers that have fed
the Law from its beginnings. Remember how the Law's reflexive
response to disruptive influences of whatever kind is to take a
tighter grip? Law wants love to answer to rational constraints,
and so answers Love's call by immediately talking about the
need for prudent (prudish) response, warning about the dangers
of opening the floodgates or starting down a slippery slope (both
metaphors pointing to the Law's pet assumption that if its control is relaxed it will be overrun by rushing emotionalism and
lose its standing). Law fears Love because Love is greater than

Law and Law knows it. And yet, if it is seen differently we might take this fear to be like fear of God, a knowledgeable fear recognizing love as a grounding force within the soul, a necessary inspiration.

The Law has managed to entrench itself against the very things that sustain and nurture love and intimacy. Fearing God-knows-what, the Law avoids getting close, ducks and covers, stepping back to get a little distance, circling, assessing the situation in terms of strengths and weaknesses, looking for a way to take charge. The Law is right that love is a disruptive force, but the perceived disruption is as much a function of the Law's habitual mental preference for stability as it is a result of love's natural proclivities. It is very hard for the Law to accept the necessity of love's woundings because the Law's rational, militaristic mind sees wounding as *avoidable,* as evidence of inadequate defenses.

If lawyers want to feel more intimacy in their lives, and I take them at their word that they do, then I suggest a practical beginning. Start small. An honest admission that, now that you ask, I'm not doing so hot today. Or including others in the small celebrations and flops of daily life and being interested in theirs. Or, if someone you know looks upset or overworked, asking how they're doing. Don't worry, it isn't prying as long as you ask from genuine concern. Why not ask?

THE CONFLICT-ADVERSE LAWYER

You'd be surprised how many lawyers are extraordinarily conflict-adverse when it comes to their personal lives. The most adversarial lawyer, one who lets no slight go unanswered, will suddenly clam up when faced with conflict in a nonprofessional setting, bending over backwards to avoid talking about anything the least disruptive or problematic.

There are many ways to look at this phenomenon. One possibility is that lawyers just get worn out from the constant exposure to conflict in their professional work. After all, the stories are everywhere about the decline of collegiality, the increase in incivility, and the growing perception of disloyalty among law firms and law departments, all of which suggests a profession embattled from within. Unfortunately, this occurs at the same time many lawyers have convinced themselves that they must assume a "tough S.O.B." stance and use scorched-earth, take-no-prisoners tactics to lure and keep clients. Caught in the metaphors of armed conflict, many lawyers have come to feel that professional life is a holding action with the enemy on all sides and dissension in the ranks. And then there is the lawyer-bashing, with its ugly, mean jokes.

No wonder lawyers want a little peace and quiet at home, safe from the front lines. After all, when soldiers come home they're supposed to be treated with tenderness and respect, right? They've been through a lot. They deserve our understanding, and they need to rest undisturbed. Right?

This theme of the returning hero has mythic appeal, and doubtless there is some truth in it. But taken too far, this USO fantasy is prone to inflation and a concomitant lack of respect for "civilians." Elevated to a higher, preferred class that is to be protected from the slings and arrows of everyday life, the lawyer can start to believe that non-professional affairs really are less important than professional ones. Even worse, the lawyer can start to wish that people who *do* care about these mundane things would keep their problems to themselves.

You see the dynamic here. The lawyer is elevated and the non-lawyer is suppressed. As the gap widens, the lawyer becomes detached and isolated amidst the euphoria of his or her inflated ideas and self-image. Meanwhile the non-lawyer grows tired of merely responding to the wants and needs of the lawyer, and resentment builds. The whole scene becomes permeated with condescension and repressed feelings of betrayal and abandonment.

Another way of looking at conflict-aversion among lawyers is based more on the subtleties of the lawyer's ideas. Often when a lawyer goes overboard to avoid conflict in his or her personal life, I find they also tend to believe they must act professionally whenever and wherever conflict occurs. In other words, regardless of where a conflict arises, the lawyer feels that he or she must respond to it *as a lawyer.* Often people will say something like "If I'm going to have all these problems at home then I might as well be at work." Such a statement indicates a mind-set in which the very appearance of conflict, regardless of setting, automatically elicits responses from the lawyer drawn from his or her professional attitudes and expectations. The Catch-22 here is that this tendency to respond to conflict by assuming a lawyering persona can often escalate the conflict. Probably every lawyer has been accused of "sounding like a lawyer" in the course of a non-professional disagreement, an accusation invariably leading to heightened hostilities. People understandably get irritated by the lawyer's shift into a lawyering persona because they perceive it to be impersonal, defensive, and possibly a strategic move on the lawyer's part to avoid or squelch the issue being discussed.

This last comment suggests the possibility that the lawyer's attempts to avoid conflict are self-defeating. The lawyer's conflict-aversion often is perceived by others as a reluctance, or inability, on the lawyer's part to get involved with everyday affairs at all. For example, imagine a male lawyer talking to his wife. She wants to talk about buying a new car, or taking a trip, or going to a movie, or whatever. But the lawyer sees each of these topics as rife with conflict. They aren't going to want the same kind of car, there's too much going on at work for him to take a trip and besides she probably wants to go somewhere too damn hot, she likes those arts films while he likes to see some action, etc. Every subject becomes a minefield. And so the lawyer just keeps quiet. If forced to respond, he does so tentatively, as if his wife were laying a trap for him. You can just imagine how this feels from the wife's perspective. It's just a matter of time before things blow up.

One also has to wonder if there really is all that much conflict in life to start with. After all, in our example the wife was just making conversation without any intention of starting trouble. Like any psychological tendency, conflict-aversion creates its own self-sustaining context. If I single-mindedly set out to avoid conflict, then I most certainly will find life to be full of potential trouble spots.

There is disruption enough in life without creating more through our own unreflective actions. One option is to redirect some of our cautious energies to be on the lookout for our own defensive attitudes. We might be alert for professional tendencies that habitually look for conflict in every situation or are otherwise blind to non-professional matters. We might try harder to respond to non-professional affairs as non-professionals. And we might stop being so hard on ourselves. Just because we're lawyers doesn't mean we have to fight every battle, ask every question, enter every debate, or solve every problem. If we can learn the limitations of our professional attitudes and responsibilities, we might find there suddenly is less conflict to be avoided.

BRIDGING THE GAP

Here's how it sometimes works. The lawyer, under the unconscious sway of the Law's mental habits, reaches an impasse in a relationship. Things are unclear and ambiguous, as the Other constantly seems to be saying one thing and doing something else. Maybe the lawyer feels his or her needs are not being respected or satisfied by the Other. A conversation ensues wherein the lawyer asks questions and makes demands, which, after all, is how the lawyer has been trained to handle situations like this. (Another favored approach of the legal mind, especially among the more "enlightened," is to *negotiate* with the Other. Negotiation is favored because of its seeming reasonableness—we both have to give and take and forge a compromise. But for the legal mind, negotiation remains a conflict of self-interests, not an opportunity for joint decision-making.) The Other answers the lawyer's questions in a manner wholly unacceptable to the lawyer, so the lawyer becomes more persistent and tries to exert more control—again mirroring how a lawyer might handle a recalcitrant or uncooperative witness. Finally the Other has had enough and begins asking a few questions of his or her own. The lawyer hears these questions as in a professional setting—as subterfuges, attempts to find the weaknesses in the lawyer's position, or outright attacks. In any event the lawyer knows better than to fall into the trap of actually responding to the Other's questions. The final lines of this doomed dialogue:

"Just a second," says the lawyer, "don't change the subject. You didn't answer my question."

"Well, excuse me," says the Other, "I didn't know I was on the *stand.*"

End of scene.

At some point in a story about a relationship gone south, lawyers often lament that the Other simply doesn't understand them, doesn't understand the pressure they are under, the demands of legal practice, or the lawyer's need to have supportive friends and family. One common way this comes up is when the married lawyer comes home after a day (and most of an evening) at the office. Maybe the lawyer's spouse also works outside the home, maybe not. The lawyer wants to unwind by telling the events of the day, not so much to inform the spouse as to get it off the lawyer's chest. At some point or another the spouse's rapt attention naturally wanders. The lawyer gets hurt and gripes that the spouse doesn't care or can't understand.

A true story. Since I stopped practicing law I have spent more time being a homemaker. I am home more than my wife, so I spend more time food shopping, cooking, and the like. One night at dinner, I remember finding myself going on and on about the fluctuation in the price of strawberries. I was really getting into it when it suddenly dawned on me how this might sound to my wife, who had just spent more than a full day at the office. But she assured me this wasn't so, her interest confirmed in both word and tone.

It might have been otherwise. She could have heard my story as pure puff, the idle talk of a mundane life. She could have assumed her professional work was more important than my economic observations about fruit and waited for a chance to interrupt with more worldly stories. She could have become bored or impatient, eyes down, picking at her food while I droned on. She could have failed to see that what I was saying *mattered to me,* that it was some of the stuff of my daily life, and not incidental stuff either. (A therapist might take awareness of strawberries as indicating a psychological move away from an abstract world composed only of legalistic concerns to a world in which strawberries also have value.)

Rarely have I heard lawyers acknowledge that they need to make more of an effort to understand the Other. There simply is too much self-indulgence within the legal mind, as if its concerns are the only ones of import, the only ones that are pressuring, the only ones of interest. One of the most disturbing distortions of the legal mind is its inability to be intuitively interested in non-legal affairs. The Law couldn't care less about my strawberries—unless I want to sue for price-fixing. This habitual neglect and disrespect of the everyday deprives the Law of countless opportunities for intimacy, love, beauty, and pleasure.

We continue to see how the Law's mental habits influence the lawyer's life. The Law expects other people to conform to it, obey its rules, abide by its desires. We have seen how the Law wants to bring its own methods and standards to bear on all of life's experiences. We know that once the Law has decided a matter it is incredibly difficult to re-open the case or to get the Law to reconsider its decision, much less overturn it. To keep things under control, the Law defines events and experiences in its terms, just as law students are taught to apply the law to the facts, and if there are any facts left over after assembling the case according to the Law's instructions they are unnecessary and can be tossed away.

So we have a multi-tiered oppression going on. First the Law demands that the lawyer conform to the Law's predilections. Then the lawyer wants the Other to conform to the lawyer's predilections, which in large part reflect the Law's demands on the lawyer. In other words, the Law reaches through the lawyer to the Other, which is one reason the Other often experiences the Law as a threat to the Other's relationship with the lawyer. When the Other hears the Law's words come from the lawyer's mouth, the Other rightly fears *for the lawyer.* It is like hearing a zealot mindlessly mouth the words of some Higher Authority. We begin to wonder where the person has gone. "Ever since you became a lawyer . . ." are the opening words of so many arguments between lawyers and their friends, lovers, and family that we must take them to heart. Have we changed? Are we doing our own talking? Has the seamless web spread too far, ensnaring all of life in its spun symmetry, holding it there while it tires from struggle? Who or what is the spider? Who or what has been caught?

There are other considerations as well. Many lawyers work long and incredibly concentrated hours. From their first waking thought to their last one before sleep, they fret and think and plan about their cases. At the office they must constantly be "on," answering phone calls from often conniving people, vigorously defending causes they don't particularly care about, dealing with competitive and political intrigues—these are the lawyer's facts of life. The lawyer develops a professional style for handling these facts, and it is nigh on impossible to turn off that style at the drop of a hat. Here is the dilemma: If lawyers stay locked within the confines of professionalism, then they suffer the ensuing personal consequences; but when they drop their professional defenses they feel exposed and vulnerable, the very things they have worked so hard to avoid.

III

Mary, twenty-nine, is a rising star at a large firm. She's a good lawyer and has a tough, uncompromising professional demeanor that has earned her a reputation, despite her youth, as a formidable adversary and a hard negotiator. She takes justifiable pride in her work and is confident that she will make partner when the time comes.

"So, what brings you to see a therapist?"

She looks at me with steady, unyielding eyes. There is a defiance in her look that seems to say, "There is nothing bothering me." And yet, here she is. After a period of studied silence she says:

"My career is going great. But," her gaze diverts to a point in the air halfway between us as if something were hanging there, "I just broke up with a man I've been seeing for several months. I thought things were going along just fine, but all of a sudden Roger said he was tired of playing second fiddle to my career."

"Was he? Playing second fiddle I mean?"

"Of course not. He just couldn't understand the demands that I'm under at work. I billed over 2300 hours last year, and this year is even tougher. I have to beef up my marketing efforts. And then I have my committee work for the bar association. Of course I'm tired when I get home. What does he expect?"

"If you're so convinced it's his fault, what's the problem?"

"Well, this isn't the first time this has happened. In fact, since I started law school I haven't really had a long-term relationship. They seem to last a few months and then just fade away. Men just can't accept me as a professional. I think they're jealous of my success."

There is a good chance Mary is correct, that the here-and-gone nature of her relationships is a function of widespread discrimination against working women, especially professionals. Another possibility is that Mary's situation also has something to do with her own personality. Most likely, there are big doses of both at work. But there is another level of psychological experience that goes beyond social bias and individual personality. Nearly one-third of lawyers report feelings of inadequacy and inferiority stemming from problems with interpersonal relationships, and my hunch is that this figure is much higher. In any event, Mary's story is being enacted nationwide by men and women alike as lawyers find themselves alone in the midst of professional success. Something basic is going on.

We have seen how the legal profession is demanding more

and more from its practitioners. Required billables rise yearly, threatening to swamp the lawyer's life, firms demand that associates and partners alike spend more of their ever-dwindling time marketing their services, collegiality is giving way to competition as associates vie for partnership spots and partners compete for survival and success, problems with civility abrade already frazzled nerves, and all of this in a break-neck technological world of instant faxes, late-night conference calls, and whirring word-processors. It is not surprising that lawyers feel like they simply have nothing left to give.

Given these harsh realities, telling Mary to spend more time on her non-legal life and less at work sounds unrealistic, if not impossible. (The extent to which lawyers appease themselves with the notion of "quality time" is one indicator of how lawyers cannot see giving more *actual* time to personal affairs as a plausible prospect.) Even worse, posing the matter to Mary in terms of "either-or" would merely reinforce the very opposition we are trying to break down. The real challenge is for Mary to find more encompassing and diverse ways of imagining lawyering itself, of seeing lawyering as part of a community, one among many, retaining its own imaginal integrity while also respecting that of others. Too many lawyers cross off their non-legal lives like a chore that doesn't really need doing, or try to make do with casual, non-committal affairs, or simply go it alone in a monastic dedication to profession.

In my experience, spouses, friends, and lovers are far more sympathetic to the lawyer's plight than many lawyers believe. They often have a deep understanding of the nature and toll of the professional demands placed on lawyers. Very often they also are more adept than the lawyer at identifying when the Law is exerting undue influence over the lawyer's life. (This probably is necessarily so because the lawyer is by nature more unconscious of the Law's influence, more blind to the Law as Unseen Mover.) Although the lawyer's friends and family might not exactly comprehend the intense pressure of daily practice, they have one huge reflective advantage over the lawyer—they get to look at the lawyer, to see the results of the Law's demands in the lawyer's taut face, tired eyes, and three drinks before dinner.

When people in relationships with lawyers say they want the lawyer to spend more time with them, they usually mean they want the lawyer to pay more attention. It is the lawyer's psychological detachment more than any literal clock-time absence that the Other feels most acutely as disinterest and abandonment. "He's here but not here" is a common description of the lawyer's absent-mindedness. No wonder so many friends, lovers, and family members come to feel like they are playing second fiddle to the lawyer's career.

The hell of it is that lawyers insist that relationships are of paramount importance to them and that trouble with relationships is the source of their greatest pain. If so, then why is this importance not being communicated to others?

Relationships in the context of legal practice are characterized if not by outright adversity then certainly by caution and circumspection. Typically, the lawyer sees professional relationships in terms of "sides" in a competition. The lawyer wants something specific from the other side and believes the other side wants something from the lawyer's side. It is assumed that anything the other side wants is antagonistic to the wants of the lawyer's side. If the lawyer's side is going to give something up or "make an admission," then the other side has to pay in kind. *Although such thinking might make sense in an adversarial context, it is poisonous to intimate relationships.* One hears echoes of this militant professionalism from the spouse who complains that the lawyer is aloof and distant, from the old friend who notes the lawyer—whom he doesn't see as much as he used to—has become more guarded and deliberative since becoming a lawyer, and from the lover who hears in the lawyer's questions the bluff and insecurity of cross-examination.

Mary's comments are typical and suggest that she has allowed professional attitudes (adversity, competition) to bleed over into her non-professional affairs. In Mary's telling, her relationships end either because a partner expects too much, or because "men" (note the categorical reduction of discrete individuals into a suspect class) are jealous of her success. She might be exactly right, but her style of thought and choice of language, indeed the very fact she is imagining in terms of "causes," suggest that Mary is trying to understand her personal relationships in terms gleaned from her professional life.

Mary has to find a way not to treat her personal relationships as if they were professional ones. She has to reaffirm her non-legal, experiential wisdom. She already *knows* that relationships with friends, lovers, and family are far more indirect and fragile than those with opposing counsel; she just has to remember what she knows. She has to recognize her hard-hitting legal style *as a style,* and be more careful about where she uses her professional tools, thereby avoiding the screw-ups that always come when using the wrong tool for the job. What works in the courtroom will not necessarily work in the more complex and delicate matters of the heart. Mary must be more willing to suspend her lawyerly penchant for clarity, structure, and stability and to accept relationships as they are—notoriously confusing, messy, mysterious, and wonderful affairs.

A final point about Mary's case. Her distress almost certainly is exacerbated by subtle sexist pressure that wrongly expects women to be primarily responsible for relationships. Men and women alike obviously need to take a close look at their attitudes about relationships to ferret out any unconscious biases about men and women's respective roles. Even better would be to set aside the notion of roles altogether. Things are difficult enough without allowing tired and threadbare expectations to make matters worse.

CHAPTER SEVEN
STAYING AND GOING

MANY LAWYERS are leaving the legal profession. Some by choice, some not. Many other lawyers are not leaving. Some lawyers find great satisfaction in their work. Others muddle through, not particularly satisfied but not dissatisfied either. Still others wish they could leave but feel they can't.

Such statements are true of any profession, I suppose, but they are particularly charged when applied to the legal profession. The Law's psychological attitudes toward its work have broader societal dimensions and present in magnified form themes running throughout society.

COPE OR QUIT

A lawyer came to see me once and said he was unhappy with his work. Why? Because he was being asked by his firm to do things he felt were unethical. What did he want from counseling? To become "better adjusted" (his words) so he could be happier at his job. Problem? The things his firm was asking him to do *were* unethical.

Another lawyer complained of being discriminated against within her firm because she was a woman. What did she want from counseling? To develop her "coping skills" (her words) so she could better "accept" her situation. Problem? She *was* being discriminated against.

In both cases, I asked the lawyers what they would do if they could not adjust, cope, or learn to accept. Both saw only one alternative. They could quit. Cope or quit—now *there's* a depressing choice.

I see the same pattern again and again in my work: People sense, rightly, mind you, that they are working in a hostile environment; then, through an introspective conversion they decide that the environment is a reflection of their own personal psychology. Answer? They must either learn to change themselves so they can accept the environment or get out. It makes such perfect sense once that subtle introversion is made. Getting better adjusted, coping, accepting—what do they mean? I take them as buzz words of a pseudo-therapy I find particularly useless and more than a little destructive.

Let's focus on our two lawyers. Their problem was that all avenues of imagination were closed to them except Cope or Quit. For example, neither of them gave any consideration to staying and trying to make things better. I don't mean they considered their options and decided it wasn't worth the effort to change things, or that they simply felt outnumbered or outgunned. I mean that the very *idea* of working to change a bad situation didn't even occur to them. And this in two highly competent professionals who were used to advocating positions, taking hard stands, and fighting for a viewpoint. How could it be that so obvious an alternative as staying and, if necessary, fighting for what was right could be so completely overlooked?

There are always numerous answers. It's possible that the sheer magnitude of the adverse conditions was so great as to not even permit the idea of change for the better. It's no use, it's too big, too powerful, there's nothing I can do, you can't change the system, it's like this everywhere. Cynical surrender is so easy. It's also possible that the lawyers' childlike helplessness was a return of their repressed vulnerabilities, fears, and weaknesses. How much the lawyers' response reminds one of a pitiful dynamic often found in child abuse: "I'll be better," cries the boy to his abusive parent, as if the parent's violence were justified by or in reaction to some shortcoming of the child. Once speaking from the place of the child (a therapeutic attitude peddled like snake-oil nowadays) of course one is going to feel small, powerless, and responsible. Either be a better boy or run away from home. It rarely occurs to children to advocate for a better life.

Much has been written about the current culture of victimization. "Dysfunction," which sounds like it should identify an anomaly, has become a normative standard. The question no longer is whether you have been abused or victimized but in what way and to what degree. Even abusers are seen as victims. The therapeutic responses growing from this belief are predictably introverted. Touch our scars, feel again the attack and wounding, deal with our feelings, own our emotions, heal our inner child, transcend the pain, and so on.

There is a related problem. Another subtle psychologism at the heart of American society preaches that the best life is one sailed in calm, protected waters. Under this view, you shouldn't rock the boat. If you're feeling a little sick, just keep it to yourself so as not to upset the other passengers. Bigotry is a squall line best avoided, but, if overtaken by it, batten down the hatches and ride it out. This smiley-face complacency would as soon not be reminded about problems or the fact that we have responsibilities to correct them. Here, too, we detect a childlike naïvete, looking at the world through kitten eyes.

I keep talking about psychology because if our two lawyers have been victimized by anything it is by reigning psychological themes like adjustment, coping, and acceptance. Applied indiscriminately, these are ideas that "disempower" people, not ones that free them.

The male lawyer decided to quit. For him it wasn't worth the hassle to stay. As for the woman lawyer, something quite remarkable happened. We spent a lot of time talking about possible political alternatives to her situation. We talked about the people involved, the power structures of her firm, the pressure points that might be susceptible to concentrated political effort. Sometimes we were downright Machiavellian. Sometimes idealistic as freshmen. But most of the time we talked about practical moralities and political possibilities and plotted ways to change things for the better. She was, after all, a highly accomplished lawyer, very sensitive to political considerations, very savvy in her understanding of personalities and their impact on things, the existence of power groups, etc. And as a professional woman, she also had a lifetime of experience with discrimination to bring to bear on her current situation.

As we talked about all of this, I noticed a change in the person I was talking to. It is hard to describe because it was more in her tone of voice, carriage of body, and intensity of eye. She seemed more like, well, an adult. Involved in a reinvigorated political imagination, her childlike plaintives were replaced with adult perspectives.

The therapeutic point is that when she activated her adult attitudes, experiences, and skills she expanded the childlike alternatives of Cope or Quit to include staying and working for change: political activism as a psychological necessity. After all, the initial obstacle stopping the two lawyers was the wrong, wrong, wrong belief that bad situations *always* reflect personal psychology. That belief was the bedrock of their passivity. What they needed was a renewed affirmation of their adult capabilities.

This is a trend. The attrition of good, competent lawyers from the legal profession is fueled in significant part by the Cope or Quit ideology. This must change. For one thing it supports the continuance of immoral and dehumanizing practices and beliefs. Cope or Quit—what could be a better way of ensuring the future of oppression and discrimination? Why do well over half of all lawyers complain that the legal profession is denying them time on this earth with friends, lovers, family, and themselves and yet things keep getting worse? Why? Too many lawyers say it's because of the client, of course—the Great Parent, Giver of Life and Rules, nurturing breast and phallocentric authority all in one. But we have played that tune enough. Blaming the client for the disarray of the legal profession distorts the actuality of both client and lawyer and tinges their relationship with inappropriate familial tensions. Surely clients are not acting *in loco parentis*, like parents.

And lawyers are not children. They are, among other things, professional thinkers, tacticians, political advisors, active defenders of freedom and justice. And yet they seem unable to apply these talents in caring for their own house and community. I would encourage the legal profession to engage in an imaginal dialogue, as the woman lawyer did with her adult capabilities. For example, instead of petulantly viewing clients as authoritarian adversaries, perhaps lawyers could see them more realistically in adult, political terms. Clients are simply as involved with their own work as we are with ours and are similarly focused on their own needs. I don't believe clients want lawyers to work too hard or to act brutishly. And if they do? Well, then they must be reminded that they will get better representation from lawyers who are enjoying more of life's fullness than work alone can provide. Adults, especially a *majority* of adults, don't have to work themselves to death in their own profession. We don't have to retain outmoded systems that favor litigation over peace-making. And adults don't have to treat other people shabbily just because somebody else tells us to.

THE MYTH OF JOB DEVELOPMENT

Another psychological perspective that weakens the individual is the myth of development. This myth proclaims we are developing, becoming beings, always growing, progressing, evolving, advancing, forever onward and upward. The myth of development is a dominant myth of our age, and one the legal profession has swallowed hook, line, and sinker. Much has been written about the golden aspects of development; commensurately less about its insidious and debilitating consequences.

Within the context of the legal profession, the issue of development is most explicitly raised with regard to career or job development. The "continuing legal education" and "human resource" industries love the idea of job development, especially because their livelihoods depend on perpetuating the myth. In both circles, the rap is always the same: If lawyers *knew* more, had more training, attended more seminars, and listened to more tapes, they could *become* more efficient, more productive, better marketers. Job development as a management tool places the lawyer under enormous pressure, constantly threatening the lawyer with the invisible specters of incompetence and obsolescence.

It is impossible to talk about, or against, the idea of job development without first recognizing it as part of the pervasive myth of development. Developmental models permeate almost all of our intellectual disciplines. Walk into any Psych 101 class and you will be taught developmental psychology: Children do this by age two, that by age four, if they can't do this by age six then they're "slow" or "maladapted" (translation: they don't fit the developmental model being applied to them). Go next door to the biology department and you will be told that life is essentially evolutionary. Up and down the hall, political scientists talk about "developing nations" and anthropologists talk about "developing cultures." History is said to be nothing but development, and some physicists say the universe is expanding still.

Things are no better off campus. Meditation cults and the

self-help brigade preach the glories of "personal development" while competing tooth and nail for the consumer's self-help dollar. At work, the lawyer is constantly harangued about "chances to develop his or her skills" and bombarded by demands to work harder on "developing business." At home, the lawyer is encouraged to work on developing good interpersonal relationships. You get the picture. Development is no longer simply a theory but has become an obsessive ideology.

That we believe in the myth of development so completely and without question is a red light if ever there was one. The problem is that the myth of development deprives us of the present. By insisting that things are always supposed to be getting better, it implies that now is never good enough. We can always be fitter, thinner, smarter, richer. When a loving and devoted spouse who has stood beside the lawyer for years is suddenly found lacking because (the lawyer says with a condescending sigh) the lawyer has "grown," the developmental myth is in the wings, applauding.

Developmental ideology has thoroughly infected the legal profession. Consider the poor law student walking into his or her first contracts class. What does the budding lawyer carry along with his or her books? A crushing burden provided by the developmental myth. Before the law student has ever opened a book or read a case, the placement office, career consultants, job manuals, and the profession in general have already defined the proper path: good grades/law review/interviews/summer job/offer/associate/partner/corner office. Before the law student has a chance to learn anything about the Law itself, developmental thought replaces present opportunities with future expectations, thereby pretty much snuffing out any hope the law student might have had of actually enjoying legal education in and for itself. Everything becomes a rung on a ladder that must be climbed. The myth of development then closes its loop by claiming that if a lawyer doesn't make it to the top it's because of poor training in the early days. Development says we aren't good enough now and need to develop, while at the same time insisting that all we are now is a result of our development to date. Here and now becomes an abstraction caught in the twin jaws of past and future as developmental thought falls into dual preoccupations, either re-shaping history or planning for tomorrow.

Developmental thought also undermines learning by denying it immediacy. Nobody says to the hapless law student: "Learn contract law because it represents an age-old struggle to shield ourselves from uncertainty. Listen carefully to the deep, binding concerns that contracts are really about: of making offers and looking for acceptance, of how lasting agreements depend on mutual consideration, of how difficult it is to reach accord and find satisfaction, and how painful are broken promises. Contractual language as soul-talk! Open your book and travel to the Four Corners where Minds come to Meet. Read there the tragedies and comedies of life's endless variations, stories of divine happenings, and of unforeseeable *forces majeure*. Learn as well the necessary techniques and odd habits of the legal craft. Master its magical language. Become conversant in its terms of art."

No, development ignores the poetry and art of legal education and cuts to the chase: "Get the grades or forget the corner office."

Development implies that we know what we need and when we need it. But we don't. The failure fully to recognize this fact is at the heart of many job development complaints. A third-year associate bemoans spending so much time reviewing documents. He is quite sure his development is lagging behind that of his peers and is concerned that it might hurt his partnership chances down the road. But so what if he has spent the last three years reviewing documents and hasn't taken a single deposition? Maybe fate has something in store for him twenty years from now when the skills he learns today will make all the difference. Or maybe not. Who knows? My question is why should the third-year associate do a good job now? So he can get a "better" job later? Or because the present job is worth doing well in its own right? Obviously the two are not exclusive, but I find increased and excessive accent placed on the former. I remember attending my first class meeting as an associate in a large firm. None of us had even passed the bar yet, but our main topic of discussion, the thing we were most concerned about, was MAKING PARTNER! Such is the curse of the myth of development. And we wonder why lawyers get depressed.

About that class meeting: It was a good example of how the myth of development subtly perpetuates class bigotry. Under the sway of developmental thought, lawyers are reduced to being second-year associates, or mid-level partners, or thirtysome-things, or a Double Income No Kids, or twenty-five- to forty-year-old consumers. Only by classifying us according to "stage" or "phase" can developmental thought keep us under its control. Classifying also helps in implementing developmental theories, because it is much easier to deal with a homogeneous group you can put through pre-set programs than to come face to face with a group of individuals. The concept most foreign and antithetical to developmental thought is that of the individual. Why? Because individuals are eccentric and developmental theories can't handle eccentricity.

Instead of fretting about what we think we're missing, we could try embracing what we have. Instead of devoting ourselves to *becoming* we might try *being* for a change. If our assignment is to look for a needle in a haystack, why not search for it with style and grace? One way to do this is to imagine that *what we are doing now is what we will be doing always*. Then, like settling into a new home, we could begin to explore the nooks and crannies of our present job, to rearrange things to suit our particular style, to love the familiar places and smells and sounds, maybe even to find happiness there. The myth of development ignores the fact that if we live for tomorrow we will certainly be dead on arrival.

Job development shares another endearing trait with developmental ideology in general—it always provides a ready scapegoat when things go wrong. Like the developmental myth in general, job development makes a scapegoat of the past. If I am troubled now, it is because I had trouble as a child. If I screw up a deposition, it's because that aspect of my job development was neglected when I was starting out. Ignorance can always be placed at someone else's doorstep, whether it's a contracts teacher or a previous employer. I cannot be a bad marketer because I find marketing demeaning, it must be because I haven't been properly trained. One of these days, after a few more seminars, you just look out.

Development deprives us the impact of our experiences by smoothing them out along a learning curve. An illusion fostered by hindsight, the myth of development actually believes in the patterns it imposes on the past and projects into the future. But life does not just develop, life also *is*. Unfortunately, once we're caught on the conveyer belt of developmental ideology, everything is expected to fuel the machine of tomorrow.

THE LONGING OF SUCCESS

John walked in and sat down across from me. He was a young man in his early forties, with thoughtful creases marking a brow just starting to show the crazings of age. On the phone his voice had sounded like a prolonged sigh, and when he spoke now his words lacked interest in themselves.

"I don't know what's wrong," he began flatly. "The other day I was coming back to the office after having lunch with one of my clients; I was riding up in the elevator, and all I could say to myself was 'Is this all there is?'"

He was quiet for a second and then continued. "I mean, there isn't any reason for me to feel this way. I've made it. I've gotten everything I ever wanted. I got into the law school I wanted and ended up getting the job I wanted, too. I made partner two years ago. But now I feel like I'm at a dead end. It just isn't enough."

I had heard variations on John's story many times. Increasingly, the path to becoming a successful lawyer is seen as a series of clearly defined goals leading to a given reward. Then the reward comes and suddenly there are no longer prescribed goals. After the blush of achievement wears off, a sense of finality and loose-endedness sets in. In the career setting, this often happens at about the time people reach an age where they start to reexamine their lives. Just when things are supposed to be good, the bottom drops out. Dead end.

It is a mistake to dismiss John's complaint as burn-out, a mid-life crisis, or simple self-indulgence. In my experience, the sense of longing John describes is widespread in the legal profession and can be profoundly troubling. Part of the trouble is the longing's undefinable quality; we need but know not what. We are flushed with desire, but there is no precision to our desire. Wantonness threatens.

Listen to how John identified the salient points of his legal career. "I've *gotten* everything I *wanted*. I *got* into the law school I *wanted* and ended up *getting* the job I *wanted*. I *made* partner two years ago." He is telling his history in terms of acquisitions—got, want, made. They rise up like stones from the water, glistening but separate. John's life has been fixated on goals, every plateau a platform from which to begin the next climb, every stop a go. All of his goals have been finite and the road clearly marked. But suddenly he finds himself in strange territory without compass or destination. What is missing in this telling are the very things that John longs for: a sense of connectedness, relation, perhaps even meaning and purpose.

The single-minded drive toward taking the next hill permeates legal practice and is responsible for many of its distresses. It can be as subtle as not hearing what a witness says because you are already thinking about the next question, or as overt as ignoring the needs of family, friends, and personal health in the head-long charge for partnership or promotion.

The word "goal" originally meant "to hinder" or "impede," and may once have meant "a stopping place." These archaic meanings suggest a counterintuitive notion that John's *goals* might be hindering him. The goals by which he marks his life may be the very things impeding his ability to enjoy his success. Let's be clear here. We aren't talking about stopping to smell the roses, we're talking about stopping and not being *able* to smell them. Taking time isn't the problem. John's goals are what have left him anesthetized.

When John asks, "Is this all there is?" what does he mean? What is the "this"? Does he mean the daily interaction with his partners and associates, taking phone calls from clients and opposing counsel, reviewing billings, handling the many little personnel (personal) problems that pop up continuously, revising and editing memoranda and letters—in short, all of the small tasks comprised by legal practice? If so, one has to wonder what he expected in the first place. Of course this is all there is. What else could there be?

Goal-directed thinking is part of the developmental trap sketched out above, and, like developmental thought in general, it ignores the here and now. Propelled by our quest for future goals, it is very hard to appreciate what is here at hand. It's like a vacationer so intent on photographing every scene that he never *sees* for himself. One wonders how he would feel if the pictures didn't turn out.

I am not saying John shouldn't have goals but that those goals need to be tempered by more intense involvement in the present. Everyone knows that working hard for the sake of future reward has a different feel to it than working for the sake of the work. There is an intimacy in the latter that is denied to the former. In the latter case, the doer wants to do right by the task, to fulfill its present needs. In return, the task gives manifest form to the doer's talents and desires. This kind of intimacy rests on mutual love and respect—we love and are loved by our work.

John needs a fuller fantasy of work and life if it is ever to be "enough." What if he concentrated more on the craft of his profession than on its potential for resumé entries? On the practice of law as a learned craft warranting attention in and of itself. No lofty ideals or pretensions, just the simple artistic demand to do the job right because the job deserves it. Suddenly he might find himself more respectful of work, more drawn to it, interested in it, returning again and again to get it just right. This kind of approach takes as much pleasure in honoring present needs as in fulfilling future expectations. By paying more attention to the vicissitudes of everyday practice, John might begin to free himself from the frustrated egotism of his goal-directed ambition. Who knows, this might even be a step toward rekindling the romance that drew him to the law in the first place.

COMING TO TERMS WITH LOSS AND FAILURE

In this chapter we have seen three ways in which lawyers have bad relations with their work. They feel helpless to change a bad situation and start thinking in terms of Cope or Quit. Or they succumb to the myth of development and are denied the present. Or they come to see their present position as the end of the line. The developmental myth actually flows through all three, the first and last being tributaries of the second. Each in its own way describes a developmental aberration, a place where the developmental myth gets stuck or turns back on itself. The clearest evidence that such work disorders are outgrowths of the myth of development are the prescriptions given by Dr. Development itself: take charge of your life, stop fighting everything and learn how to get along better, set yourself some realistic goals and then steadily work toward them (don't shoot too high or you might be disillusioned—as if every failure to arrive were the fault of the traveler), *there are always new challenges to be met.* This last one is a real kicker—the old "will to live" doctrine re-tooled by the myth of development and put to work in the name of perpetual productivity. Never stop, there is always more to do. If you stop you become obsolete, in the way, dead wood, organizational fat. Watch out, because once you lose the will to go on, to grow, to progress, to produce you'll go into decline and might even die. As if declining were not every bit as natural as ascent.

We come now to one of the cruelest aspects of the developmental trap. In a society addicted to development and becoming, there is little room for loss and failure. It's funny, we're always going somewhere but we have no commensurate fantasy of what we are leaving. Perhaps this is because ours is a land of new arrivals, fresh beginnings, of starting over and making a clean break with the past. Religious outcastes, political heretics, economic refugees, people just seeking a better life—all of these pioneers live in our national soul. But missing to a significant degree in all of this is a strong feeling for one's failures or an appreciation for what's being left behind. In our national mind, failure is just a place to start the story. Rags to Riches. But there is great value in loss and failure. When we experience loss and failure, they intensify our awareness of other losses, other failures. But more important, they establish for us that loss and failure are psychological necessities. In any event, nobody gets through life without them.

Let's look at it in terms of losing a job. Every job eventually comes to an end, whether that means getting fired, moving on by choice, retirement, or whatever. The operative word is *loss*. Even if we switch jobs without actually getting fired, even if we hate the job we leave behind and love the one we find, the fact remains that we are leaving behind something that has been an informing part of our life. It is this sense of loss that must be respected, even savored.

III

A man of fifty-five has reached a point of comfortable retirement. He says the luster went out of practicing law years ago, and he has been looking forward to getting out of the rat race. In fact, the seductive image of retirement has been the only thing keeping him going the last few years. One more month and Free at Last!

He is having dreams like you wouldn't believe. "I can't explain it," he says. "I've never had dreams like this. In fact I hardly ever remember my dreams at all. Why should this be happening now, at the happiest time of my life?" The problem for him is that there is much death in his dreams. Murders occur, although in the disinterested way they sometimes do in dreams. In his dreams are visages of people long forgotten; of his dead grandparents, who died separately many years apart and whom he never knew as a couple; of scenes that seem like montages of homes once inhabited and places once visited—a room in a house where he once lived, for example, appears as an office suite thirty floors up. The overall atmosphere of his dreams is one of confused frustration, not fear or dread, but a more simple anxiety akin to having something on the tip of your tongue. It's as if he knows what is going on but can't put it into words, can't "explain it" (as he himself put it in describing his waking relationship to these dreams; note how the dream's imaginal style recurs in his telling).

Who knows what such dreams mean? But it is safe to say they are describing a world not entirely intent on his happy retirement. They seem to be going over things left behind, hoisting them up from the well of memory and re-presenting them in collective and transposed forms. While his dayworld consciousness is full of life and new beginnings, his dreamworld is filled with death and historical recapitulations. Are his dreams suggesting that such things are necessary accompaniments to his dayworld sense of new beginnings? Are they raising the very issues that will involve him when he retires? After all, they come to him after he retires at night. Maybe his dreams have nothing to do with his impending retirement, but they certainly are providing him with a deep reflection missing from his anticipatory dayworld stance. One has to wonder how his dreams might change if he gave these reflective themes more conscious attention. Is it just incidental that "reflect" means "to bend back" while "retire" means "to pull back"? Isn't one part of retirement the writing of one's memoirs? One cannot find memories in the future; one must go back for them; one must imagine in past tense.

I take these dreams as evidence of the fundamental importance of loss and failure to psychological life. Applied to the job setting, this means that when leaving a job, regardless of reason, a person must *engage the emotions of departure*. These emotions are essential to loss and may be its most psychologically significant aspect. Each of us will suffer departure and loss differently, but certain recurring feelings do seem to attach themselves to moments of loss—feelings like grief, loneliness, sorrow, and dark thoughts of mortality and death.

Too many times, we erect barriers to such feelings. One of the strongest lines of defense is betrayal. Especially in situations where we have been fired or have become disillusioned with our work, it is difficult to escape the bitter taste of betrayal. "They weren't honest about what they expected when they hired me," we say. Or, "They never told me they weren't satisfied with my performance." Or, "I'm a better lawyer than Jones will ever be, but they didn't fire *him*. I guess I just didn't kiss up to the right people." And so on. Betrayal defends against rejection by trying to turn the tables: I'm not the one who is inferior. Hey, it's *their* loss, we say.

Sometimes, of course, we *have* been betrayed, we *were* lied to, factors other than our skills *did* contribute to an unjust decision to let us go. But the issue is not so much whether or not we were actually betrayed, but that the sense of betrayal continues to betray us by not letting us let go. Make no mistake about it, a feeling of betrayal is a disguised attempt to maintain the old connections. A feeling of betrayal militates against the direct experience of loss that is necessary for resurrection of the spirit, and therefore betrays our own chance at self-renewal. As long as I remain trapped in feelings of betrayal, as long as I condemn my boss for betraying me, the longer he or she will remain my boss, and the longer the betrayal will hold me.

Closely aligned with betrayal is cynicism. "They're all bastards. This is the last time I depend on anybody else. From now on I'm looking out for number one." Such comments, usually uttered beneath the breath and with a sideways glance, are generally statements of impotence and helplessness. Show me a person who says he or she doesn't need anybody and I'll show you a soul in need. At its worst, cynicism tries to protect the injured part of us by isolating and shielding it from further harm. We stop loving or trusting or needing—and the soul withers. Cynicism becomes *self*-betrayal, and once again distracts us from the essence of our loss.

Another common way we deprive ourselves of the sense of loss that comes with losing a job is through self-deprecation. No longer employed, we feel cut out, discarded, remnants of our former selves. It is hard to imagine anyone not feeling this way given the circumstances, which are trying. But sometimes we take a false step and equate losing a job with being a failure. Consider an analogy. Imagine falling in love. You date for months, maybe years, and at last you pop the big question and the beloved says No. Worse, he or she suggests that perhaps you should begin to see other people. You are devastated. Maybe you feel betrayed. Maybe you vow never to love again. Or maybe you lapse into self-pity and conclude you just weren't good enough. But to say you are a failure because the one you have chosen decides not to choose you is to shift responsibility for your identity onto the other person. What appears on the surface to be selfless immolation turns out to be plain, ordinary selfishness. Like betrayal and cynicism, self-pity is just another way of denying the significance of our losses and failures.

Our lives are as much a story of our losses as of our achievements. The soul needs our losses at least as much as our successes, sometimes even seems to prefer them, as if losses are sources of the soul's deepest and most resolute strengths. Is it not in times of loss that we find out who our real friends are, who and what we can really depend on? Think about how the importance of friends and family re-emerges in loss, and how often the very ties we have neglected become the bonds that hold us together in times of loss. *Loss provides a place where love and dependence can reside.* Appreciating this place is far more important than submitting to the misguided accusations of betrayal and cynicism or the hollow vanity of self-pity and defeatism.

Loss is painful. Those dark moments at three in the morning when we awaken alone and anxious, staring at the ceiling and wondering if dawn will ever come, our demons loose and at us— these are not moments to seek out. The point is not to dwell on loss but to engage it. The idea is to greet the emotions when they come, to respect their expression, to listen and be interested in what they have to say. What are we mourning? Is it the money? The prestige? The comfort of familiar surroundings? What? If we recall that every loss depends on a pre-existing bond, then these emotions and images can become our truest guides in telling us exactly what we have lost, which might turn out to be very different from what we think.

Just as loss requires attachment and connection, failure requires expectation. In a highly personalized and self-preoccupied culture such as ours, such expectations tend to be personal in nature. We sit down to draw a picture of a horse and when it doesn't turn out we tend to focus on our feelings of inadequacy as an artist. But to the extent that our sense of failure is heightened by our own egotism, there is little to do but recognize our grandiosities and get over them.

There are, of course, personal feelings of failure not tied to inflated self-image. Sometimes we simply feel inadequate. Well, yes, so we are. So what? We *must* be inadequate because the ideal of success is just that, an ideal transcending mortal capabilities. For that matter, mythology is full of stories about gods who fail.

By recognizing failure as necessary we can respect its significance while also seeing it as no big thing. The fall into failure is greatly exaggerated, overstated as it must be by the high-flying perspectives of success and perfection. A more down-to-earth view of failure might see how failure helps to identify natural limitations. Nothing is better than failure for reminding us of the difference between humility and humiliation.

Failure is not in the first instance a personal matter. It is the drawing of the horse, after all, that didn't turn out. This is a fine point, but a significant one. *By critiquing our personal feelings of inadequacy in terms of the failed work, we shift the perspective from ego to soul.* Instead of just sitting around licking the ego's cut and bruised pride, why not also ask about the failed work? What, exactly, failed? What's wrong with the work? Apart from my personal shortcomings, what else does the work's failure tell me? Were expectations so high to begin with that failure was inevitable? Was the conception of the work poorly framed from the start? What really went wrong?

Standards of unflagging success necessitate a continuing stream of failure. Like smoke from a rocket, failures indicate where our ambition has been, leaving a tell-tale trace of its course. This ongoing sense of failure is a natural correlate to the drive for success and perfection. In fact, looked at from the ground up, failures are the foundations on which successes are built. Failure as infrastructure. If we fail to fail, we can never be sure of our foundations and our work will be tentative, lacking in confidence. We must fail to succeed.

CHAPTER EIGHT
SOUL VALUES

IT IS MID-MORNING in old Athens and a precursor of the modern lawyer has risen to speak on behalf of a litigant. He begins his oration with a personal testament to the litigant's good character, honesty, and forthrightness. Having laid this foundation, the citizen advocate then affirms his personal belief in the rightness of the litigant's cause. He takes his seat and another citizen rises to repeat the litany—I know the litigant to be honest, his cause just, and I cast my lot with his.

In those early days (roughly the second half of the fifth and first half of the fourth century B.C.E.), it was assumed such orators were expressing their *personal* belief in both the litigant and his cause. Usually these advocates were chosen precisely because of some personal connection with the litigant. Often they were relatives, close friends, neighbors, or people from the same "club" as the litigant. In a very real sense, they were at once advocates and character witnesses, and it was therefore essential that they be willing to profess their belief in the litigant on the basis of personal knowledge and faith.

It was unthinkable for an orator to argue on behalf of a litigant without this personal conviction. In fact, payment for advocacy was seen as a form of bribery that disgraced both litigant and advocate. (Around 403 B.C.E., a statute was enacted in Athens actually *forbidding* paid advocates.) Only later, in the latter half of the fourth century B.C.E., did professional, paid representation become a common practice. The early predisposition against paid advocacy was based on a belief that it gave the rich an advantage over the poor, and that advocacy on behalf of someone you believed in was part of a citizen's duty. Under this view, paid representation degraded civic responsibility.[27]

We obviously have come a long way. The modern lawyer not only isn't seen as sharing his or her client's views and beliefs, such a correlation of belief is now considered irrelevant. Not only are lawyers not expected to be character witnesses for their clients, they aren't allowed to be even if they want to. Their job is to advocate the client's position, whatever the lawyer might personally think about it. I remember well my surprise in law school when I learned that a trial lawyer isn't allowed to express his or her personal belief in the rightness or honesty of the client or the client's position. I wasn't allowed to say, "I believe Mary is telling the truth" or "I know John to be an honorable man." Such comments, I was told, were inappropriate, objectionable, and could even lead to a mistrial. On the other hand, such prohibitions notwithstanding, it was permissible (and encouraged as good advocacy) to send these same messages subliminally. Although I couldn't say outright that I believed in John or his cause, I could stand beside him in the courtroom, my hand on his shoulder, and call him by his first name in an orchestrated attempt to show I believed he was a good fellow, honest and true.

We know lawyers tend not to like discussions about right and wrong because such discussions elude clear definition and generally are too messy to get a good hold on. They also are seen as basically beside the point because the rules of the legal profession assure lawyers that it doesn't matter whether they believe in a client's cause or not. Given this premise, it isn't a big step to assuming that it also doesn't matter whether the client's position is right or wrong in a more fundamental sense. The lawyer's job is to accept, within some parameters of course, the client's position and then to represent it as persuasively as possible. If part of that representation means using the old hand-on-the-shoulder-call-him-by-his-first-name trick, then so be it.

But we have a problem here. Despite the Law's discomfort with moral discussion, and regardless of the legal profession's mandate that lawyers be objective advocates without regard to personal belief, the lawyer's own ethical sense remains. If this ethical sense is unduly restrained or denied, then we can expect to see the results of this denial reflected in the lawyer's psychological life. Although we tend to think of ethics in more philo-sophical, moralistic terms, it is also a psychological reality that permeates all aspects of thought and action. How we think about ethics cannot be divorced from how we imagine our own souls.

III

A client arrives in the lawyer's office with the following story. A year ago the client signed a contract to purchase raw materials for the client's plant. Since then the client has found the same materials cheaper elsewhere. He wants the lawyer to find a way out of the contract. The lawyer reads the contract, talks to the client some more, and concludes that everything seems in order. In retrospect, the client could have made a better deal, but the deal was fairly negotiated and the contract appears to be legally enforceable. The lawyer also knows that this is not what the client wants to hear. What's the lawyer to do?

One answer might be to tell the client too bad. You made the deal, gave your word, and now must live with the consequences of commitment. Another answer might be to try to renegotiate the deal with the supplier. Another answer might be to hit the law books to concoct a "reasonable" argument for breaking the contract. Still another answer might be more strictly economic: Figure out the financial risks of breaching the contract versus how much the client can save by paying a lower price. If the spread is big enough, lay the groundwork, breach the contract, and take your chances. Maybe the supplier won't be willing, or able, to sue.

The average representation probably includes parts of many, if not all, of the above. And of course you can pursue several options at once. But which approach does the Law prefer?

The case comes to trial. The lawyer addresses the jury and tells a story of changing circumstances, of late deliveries and poor service. The client had no choice but to go elsewhere. "Bill" (hand-on-shoulder) tried to make the agreement work but Com-pany X's greed and intransigence simply got to be too much . . .

In his or her heart, the lawyer knows this story is plausible but untrue. If greed lies anywhere it is with the client. In fact, the lawyer knows he or she is using the legal process to thwart a legal contract.

Or *does* the lawyer know this? Lawyers habitually avoid the question of whether a client's position is right or wrong. "That's a jury question," we say, implying that it isn't the lawyer's job to make such determinations. The lawyer's job is aggressively to advocate the client's position while the other side does the same thing. The jury can decide what's right. If pressed further, lawyers have another argument: "Our legal system is based on the belief that truth will emerge through an adversarial contest. If lawyers started deciding what was right and wrong on their own, they would be setting themselves up as judge and jury. People would be deprived of legal representation." And if that's not good enough, we have a rationalization of last resort: "Besides, if one lawyer doesn't take the case another lawyer will."

This recitation is ingrained in lawyers from the minute they enter law school. They are taught that, except in extreme circumstances, personal ethical beliefs are unrelated to the obligation to provide legal representation. Even the rules governing legal practice make it difficult for a lawyer to refuse a case because he or she finds the client's cause personally objectionable, unless it is so repulsive to the lawyer as to render him or her incapable of providing full and vigorous representation.

Regardless of whether you agree with this jurisprudential approach, it has significant psychological implications. As we shall see, separating intrinsic moral responses from professional judgment is an unnatural separation at best. It goes against the grain of the ethical sense, and it can have unsettling consequences.

THE MORAL IMAGINATION

In the *Protagoras*, Plato tells a story of how humans came by their moral sense. There, two gods were given the task of distributing to each of the newly formed animals their proper qualities. Epimetheus distributed the qualities, but he forgot about the humans and gave all of the best qualities to the other animals. When Prometheus came to inspect, Plato tells us, he found "man alone was naked and shoeless, and had neither bed nor arms of defense." Prometheus did the best he could to try and rectify things. He even went so far as to steal fire and the mechanical arts from the Gods and gave them to the humans in an effort of recompense. But even these benefits were not enough. The human race faltered and retreated into mean-spirited groups. We faced extinction, and most surely would have perished but for the divine intervention of Zeus. Unable to watch our inexorable decline, Zeus gave humans the one trait they needed for survival and greatness, the gift of a moral sense. Then as now, it was not fire that saved us, or our cleverness with tools. It was our moral sense.

Ethics is bred in our bones. Some scientists have even speculated that ethics might be genetically based. Perhaps in their own way, working within the constructions of their science, they are recognizing what Plato has already told us, *that humans are essentially ethical creatures.* When Prometheus asked Zeus if the moral sense should be given only to some humans, as he had done in the manner of the arts, Zeus said no and instructed that the moral sense be distributed among *all* humans so that each might share in its saving spark.

I find it useful to think of ethics as emotion. We have to be careful here not to fall into the old debate over whether ethics is purely subjective or has objective justification beyond personal opinion. The problem with that philosophical tangle is that it ignores the *existence* of the ethical *sense* in favor of arguments over this or that ethical *position.* But I want to keep us focused on the *emotional reality* of *felt* ethical tensions.

Like other emotions, ethics seems to have a life of its own. The ethical sense arises from within us and presses itself upon our attention. Anyone who has ever been nagged by a guilty conscience knows that you can't just turn off the ethical sense like an irritating song on the radio. Ethics is *felt,* and invites from us a response. Ethical reflection, on the other hand, and the theories and laws it constructs, are always afterthoughts, tracking the elusive ethical impulse.

In Plato's telling, the other animals of the earth live through their superior cunning, adaptability, and physical prowess. Even today, animals seem to us to live more directly than we do, more in accord with their natures, more in tune with their environment. Theirs is a visceral life, a life lived from the heart; and for them things are largely as they appear to be. Ethics, in our sense of the word at least, has no place among them. Who would condemn a tiger for acting as a tiger?

But in humans, ethics creates a curious unrest. It rumbles within each of us, louder in some than others, and is immediately felt if not immediately recognized. This rumbling gives rise to a pause. Instead of direct, habitual action in the manner of

the other animals, under the sway of ethics our responses become mediated and tentative. We stop to ponder and find ourselves wondering what to do. Suddenly we are undecided, uncertain, unsure. *That* is ethics as emotion. If Plato is correct, that is
how salvation feels.

The word "emotion" comes from roots meaning *to move outward.* Through ethics we move outward, beyond selfishness and
narcissism to larger ideas of community and polis. Ethics will
not leave us alone, and that is precisely the point. Ethics always
draws us to others, creating an imaginal space where our mutual
frailties can be attended. For Aristotle, who gave us the word
"ethics," the human is first and foremost a *political animal,* a child
of the earth like the other animals, yes, but possessing a natural
endowment for compassion, altruism, and selfless conduct.

During the Enlightenment and the Romantic period, philosophers and poets began to speak anew of a "moral imagination."[28] They believed that imagination is essential to morality.
Why? Because imagination is necessary for sympathy. In this
context, sympathy is freed from its usual hand-wringing connotations and taken as a form of ethical understanding, as the
human's primary moral talent. There is something intuitively
attractive about this view. How can we put ourselves into the
shoes of another without sympathy? To think their thoughts
and feel their feelings? But what isn't as obvious is the connection between sympathy and imagination. Shelley, in *A Defence
of Poetry,* wrote that to be "greatly good" a person:

> must imagine intensely and comprehensively; he must put him-
> self in the place of another and of many others; the pains and
> pleasures of his species must become his own.

"The great instrument of moral good," said Shelley, "is the
imagination."

By insisting that imagination is ethically necessary, we re-
claim ethics on behalf of soul and begin to move away from
what has come to pass as ethics: issue-oriented arguments over
rights and responsibilities, how to define them, how to justify
them, and how best to impose them on others. We begin to see
that ethics is grounded, not in the scales of cost/benefit analysis,
or on the edge of a sword, but in the imaginative capabilities of
the soul.

Some early Greek thinkers saw ethics as "care of the soul,"

and for them the primary goal of ethics was a contented soul. Imagine. Ethics in which the paramount concern is not to vindicate a position but to do right by the soul. Ethics as *psyche-therapeia*—care of the soul. Such an ethics would call for special skills and talents. Foremost among these talents would be sympathetic understanding. We would have to be willing to refrain from the usual parries and thrusts of ethical debate and to open ourselves to another's feelings.

How different this is from a competitive ethics committed to taking sides, defending positions, and winning through strength. So often nowadays we confuse winning an argument with being right. Why are we so afraid of views that differ from our own? Why is it so hard for us to give them fair hearing? Sometimes I wonder if deep in our souls we don't remember those early days before Zeus' intervention. Is that the fear in the zealot's eye? The fear that to be wrong is to fall from grace? To no longer be fully human?

DILEMMA ETHICS

When we talk about ethics we almost always end up arguing about choosing between conflicting positions. There are two sides to every story, we say, as if there can be *only* two sides, or that we even necessarily have to think of stories in terms of "sides." Why inject this subtle adversity? Why must alternative views be seen as necessarily conflicting? Even compromise comes to be seen as a kind of hybrid choice, keeping us locked securely within the ideology of choice.

The ideology of choice, and its chip-on-the-shoulder attitude, is hard at work in how we understand and respond to ethical dilemmas. Notice how easily these two words go together: ethical dilemma. It's hard to imagine one of these words without the other one coming to mind. Given the natural affinity of these words for one another, ethical dilemmas can also be seen as implying dilemma ethics. By this I mean that we tend to understand ethics from the perspective of dilemmas, in the style of dilemmas. This tendency is encouraged by the ideology of choice and suggests that "dilemma ethics" connotes a psychological perspective, an habitual approach to ethics, a genre of ethical imagination.

The dictionary defines "dilemma" as "a situation requiring a choice between equally undesirable alternatives."[29] This definition represents a mind-set in which we are caught before we get started. There are nothing but choices and *by definition* there are no good answers.

You see how this is shaping up. First there is psychological pressure to split a given ethical situation into choices. Then the choices themselves are tinged with pessimism. No wonder we develop an aversion to ethical questions.

Given the pressure to split ethical situations into choices, we often resort to abstractions. The real-life circumstances that comprise an ethical dilemma are translated into debates between loftier, more encompassing moral positions. Actual choices become mere symbols in a transcendent contest. Abstract moralizing also helps to counteract the gloominess of being left to choose between undesirable alternatives by setting the ethical question on a more ethereal plane where we can work out a theoretical response without being tied down by the facts. And if our theory results in worsening the actual circumstances presented by an ethical dilemma? An "unfortunate consequence." But we can't let facts dictate our theory, now can we? If we did we'd be changing our theory all the time. Too uncertain.

I am describing in stark terms a kind of ethical pathology that can arise when the ethical sense is dissociated from its living participation in the world. Just listen to most ethical debates. They are quite remarkable in their lack of real-world particularity. They can be passionate arguments, but the passion is primarily directed to the argument itself and the championing of this or that narrowly defined idea. In an incredible display of intellectual reversal, the real-world circumstances presented by the ethical dilemma become *examples* used to illustrate theories of competing sides. This abstract moralizing deadens the world by removing its ethical vitality and leaves ethical questions bodiless, lacking in particularity and substance, faceless victims of warring surgeons. This style of ethical pathology sees the world's complexity as irritating, its spontaneity as troubling, and its opportunities as threats.

Trapped within the ideology of choice, dilemma ethics limits our ability to envision and craft suitable responses to ethical situations. As our dictionary definition told us, dilemma ethics sees nothing but bad options; for it negotiation is largely a matter of cutting losses. "Nobody's going to like this solution," say the politicians, implying this is a sign of a *good* solution.

But wait. Must we think of dilemmas in this way? Don't we have a choice?

"Dilemma" originally meant "double assumptions." This old meaning suggests that dilemmas perhaps have less to do with choice and more to do with revealing the duplicity of our assumptions. Instead of always taking us upward into high-minded ethical debates, perhaps dilemmas also want to draw our attention downward to the animal below the horns on which we are caught. Instead of two pointedly different possibilities, one ethical animal. Alive, placed, and aware.

These ethical animals roam the borders of religion and the outer reaches of scientific understanding. Here there is talk of life or death. But dilemmas also are at home in the more mundane affairs of everyday life. Which car to buy, where to live, when to say yes. The wide range of territory where dilemmas show up is further proof that they are part of our environment, that they live where we do, and that their success or failure is destined to be our success or failure.

Talking about dilemmas as if they were animals is just one way of reaffirming their, and our, connection to the ethical sense. Dilemmas incite the moral imagination by making us sensitive to the moral tensions embedded in life itself, like sore spots that draw our attention. After all, we are drawn to dilemmas in the first instance by their raw emotional power, a power having practical and political bearing, and indicating the return of ethics as emotion. And with this return of ethical sensitivity comes the God-given chance for sympathetic understanding.

THE CODIFICATION OF THE LEGAL MIND

Some scholars say that before the late eleventh century, the peoples of Western Europe did not distinguish between legal institutions and other, more indigenous forms of community.[30] For them the law was not a separate body of rules and regulations but an inherent part of everyday life interwoven through the social fabric.

With the advent of modern written law, a different notion of society emerged. Where once it was impossible for a person to think of himself or herself in isolation from the community, this now became the accepted view. Society began to focus more on individuals and their inalienable rights. Philosophers provided theories to suit the times, in particular declaring the individual to be *the* defining political metaphor. According to this view, communities are best understood as groups of volunteers. If an individual *chooses* to live in a community, then a "social contract" is formed, and the contract's provisions are spelled out in the fine print of statutory law.

The Law contains a curious and powerful blending of these two themes. It champions the primacy of individual rights at the same time that it steadfastly encourages spelling out the parameters of these rights. Contractualism between self-interested individuals defines the very essence of how the Law thinks about relationship. Oral contracts might be binding, but far better to spell it out in the letter of the law.

This contractual, codified approach to human interaction carries over into mainstream thinking about ethics. The problem is that an ethics based on abstract "rights and responsibilities" composed solely of individual choices cannot lead to community. Such an ethics can at best muster only utilitarian claims. Perhaps it can promise order, uniformity, and predictability— and sometimes even live up to this promise—but it cannot generate community because it lacks the ethical gift.

Ethical codes, like contracts, can be reassuring by providing a common reference point and a consensually-agreed-to stopping place for ethical inquiry. But ethical codes bring with them a range of self-sustaining assumptions that determine not only *what* game is to be played but *how* it is to be played. Under a narrowly construed codified approach (and lawyers are taught that statutes and contracts should be narrowly construed), if there isn't a rule for a particular situation then that situation is ruled out of the game. If a rule doesn't prohibit X, then it is assumed that one may *do* X. And all ties go to the code. For the codified mind, profound ethical ambiguities are replaced with more strategic considerations of what the rules will allow.

Here again we see the not-so-subtle dissociation of the ethical sense from living participation in the world. This splitting off of the ethical sense is part of our modern legacy and therefore is present to some degree in each of us. It has visible consequences, appearing in individuals and institutions alike. A prosecutor can be personally appalled by capital punishment but nonetheless argue vehemently for its application. A black lawyer can represent a Klan member, a Jewish lawyer a Nazi. In such cases a distinction is being drawn between personal ethical preferences and beliefs and larger, more encompassing moral and legal obligations. It is a social convention that public duty and private preference are severable in this fashion. Remember how John Kennedy was forced to declare publicly that his religion wouldn't interfere with his politics? In more deplorable form, this public/private, professional/personal distinction also appears when elected officials accused of wrongdoing self-righteously protest they have "broken no laws." As if that ended the matter.

There also are invisible consequences of reducing the ethical sense to abstract arguments over the meaning and application of codified rules. We know that when emotion is repressed it can return in altered, symptomatic forms. If so, why take chances by repressing the ethical sense through the strictures of codification? In extreme cases, such restrictions can result in personalities split like a difference: one personality living a guided life, full of moralism and certainty; the other personality living alone, left to its privacy, prone to moodiness and unrest. The former personality appears more stable and is readily accepted into polite society; the latter appears more eccentric, erratic, and usually is dismissed as too personal to be relevant to practical and political concerns.

Replacing the ethical sense with a strictly codified approach also can lead to ethical atrophy. I remember talking to a lawyer about whether enacting codes of professional conduct was a suitable response to problems of incivility. He agreed that such codes tend to state the painfully obvious—don't lie, don't say one thing in the hall and another in front of the judge, don't be obnoxious, etc. And yet he thought that codes of conduct should be widely enacted. Why? Because then if a client complained about the lawyer treating opposing counsel with respect, the lawyer could point to the code and say "See? I have to be respectful. It's in the rules." Here was an example of ethical atrophy. Without a code to support the lawyer's ethical impulses, they were unable to stand on their own.

As usual, the danger lies in psychological exclusivity. Ethical codes are tools, not replacements for a vital and well-exercised ethical sense. Depending strictly upon codes means that our ethical substance remains paper-thin, subject to technical manipulation and authoritative amendment. But as anyone who has written a contract can testify, it is impossible even for a God to anticipate every circumstance, to cover every base. Another approach might be to take ethical codes as only one color on a richly varied ethical palette.

RESOLUTIONS

THE FINAL CHAPTER of even a short book brings expectations of summary and resolution, of concluding remarks and sound advice on how to set things right. Lawyers, especially, want practical what-to-dos. Given such expectations, it is easy to fall into abstractions appearing nowhere in any individual, and to forsake the soul's precisely given images for detail-obliterating concepts. There also is the not-so-subtle urge to wrap things up, figure it out, and to explain things once and for all.

But given the ever-changing scene of psychological life, conclusions are always tentative. All I have said could be said differently, every image turned for new reflections. Psychological musings, therefore, and the advice they offer, are always playing catch-up, like a commuter with last month's schedule, watching from the platform as the train of thought pulls away from the station.

This said, certain themes do emerge from what we have said. One theme in particular is so common as to require special attention. It's like a recurring flavor in a cuisine. It complements, sometimes intensifies, whatever stew it's in. It isn't always there, of course, but it's there often enough to seem characteristic of the psychology of Law and lawyers that we have been sampling.

The Law and lawyers have become abstracted from the world of actual experience. That is, they are living abstracted lives, drawn away from interaction and participation. When we talk about a political debate or a business dispute and say, "The only winners in that one will be the lawyers," where "lawyers" is used as a faceless symbol, we give voice to how many lawyers feel—like actors with set parts who are never allowed to come out from behind their masks.

Whether in terms of feeling like a fungible component in a big law firm machine, or like a sideline spectator of one's own family life, or like an amoral technician servicing the bottom line, or like an impostor and fraud, lawyers feel dissociated from daily life—*including themselves*. I have heard many lawyers describe a feeling of watching their own lives, observing themselves as if there is a deep separation within them. This separation sets up an inner person, an observer, who feels independent from the lawyer's everyday, habitual self, and who seems to have a perspective on the thoughts and actions of the habitual self. In some variations on this theme, this inner observer can sometimes have religious overtones (the voice of conscience), or act as a Critic ("You're so unorganized"). But when this inner observer becomes *abstracted* from everyday life, as happens with many lawyers, it takes on a peculiar demeanor and *begins to act and feel uninterested in the life it is witnessing*. In turn, the lawyer's everyday self starts to believe it is unimportant, meaningless, mediocre. Get this. The lawyer's life is split into objective action and private thought, with each perspective *aware* of the other, and each believing that the other doesn't care about it. The *overall* psychological attitude is summed up in language shared by both perspectives: "So what?" "What difference does it make?" "It's all a game, anyway."

There is something anesthetizing and deadening about the Law's mental habits that is leaving lawyers numb to deep feeling. It isn't even so much that lawyers feel bad. No, the danger lies in their not feeling enough or at all, like a guy with no sense of touch leaning on a hot stove.

LIFE BELOW THE CLOUDS

There is another aspect of the lawyer's abstraction that isn't numb to pain. I've said that lawyers feel lonely, but it is more than loneliness. Lawyers feel exiled, rejected by their fellow citizens. This sense of exile contributes much to the psychology of lawyers, from their quiet depression to their aggressive incivility, from their defensiveness to their addictions. Lawyers can see the action, maybe even dream about getting a piece of it, yet are too often unable to touch it, to be part of it, to join in the festivities.

This sense of exile obviously is encouraged by things like lawyer-bashing and general social disregard. But there is a more subtle side to it. The lawyer's sense of exile is like a political reflection of the lawyer's abstract mind-set. Ignored by the inner observer, the lawyer's everyday life as a member of the polis starts to itself feel uninteresting, dull, and worthless. Nothing the lawyer does seems able to get much of a response from the observer, so eventually the lawyer just gives up and stops trying altogether. A vicious cycle is set up: The observer becomes increasingly uninterested in everyday life while the lawyer's everyday life becomes increasingly less interesting and more distrustful of introspection. This state of mild torpor can continue for years. Note how this state of affairs corresponds to the lawyer's common complaints of feeling inadequate and inferior on one hand and socially alienated on the other. Such symptoms are edges of the same psychological sword, a sword honed on the lawyer's professional mental habits.

Psychological life cannot be expressed, much less lived, in only abstract terms. Soulful expressions also take metaphorical and aesthetic forms, relying on sympathetic understanding and intuitive appreciation as much as on conceptual analysis and logical reasoning. Statistics might provide quantitative evidence of our commonality, that we are cohorts sharing mutual endeavors, but they cannot portray life in a manner available to soul.

Soulful expressions always seem to suggest other possibilities now unknown, a fact that irritates the Law to no end. In keeping with its abstract allegiances, the Law prefers a kind of mathematized thinking that seeks to curtail multiplicity in favor of an idealized final solution that provides predetermined ways of answering all concerns. The Law is like a grumpy physicist who believes in the inviolability of equations while bemoaning the absence of a unified theory. But there is something in the Law's anxiety that is missing in the physicist's annoyance. The Law knows that its most important work is not in pure research but in applied science. It knows it often must act before it is ready to act and before its decisions can be verified and ordained from other quarters. And, most importantly, the Law sees its work as charged with the obligations of protection. If the theoretical physicist fails, nothing very bad will happen. But the Law believes itself to be the only bulwark against anarchy. In practice, this means that the Law must continuously work to not let things get out of hand. Order must be maintained, and volatility and excess avoided at all costs. The Law therefore follows the lead of its clerical antecedents by placing itself in opposition to passion and imagination—the first as disturbing and disruptive and the latter as seditious.

Similarly, the Law's chosen emblems, the scales and the sword, suggest a natural inclination on the part of the Law to over-emphasize the importance of balance and heroic strength—note how lawyers get so uptight when they feel un-balanced or out-of-kilter, or how they tend to bluster and cover when they feel vulnerable or weak. The very things the Law tries to avoid in its abstract struggle with everyday life are what return in its own life, just as repressed passion can come back as incivil-ity and repressed emotion as ethical breakdown. An additional and unfortunate side-effect of all of this is that by trying to avoid the sudden veerings and backings of life, the Law deprives itself great opportunities for psychological insight.

The thing that upsets the Law and lawyers the most is being up-set. It's as if there is a layer of abstract disturbance that is distin-guishable from the actual events that lawyers tend to posit as the "causes" or "sources" of their distress. For example, it isn't so much that a lawyer can't talk to his or her spouse that troubles the lawyer as it is the very fact that the lawyer's life is being inex-plicably disrupted—inexplicably, that is, to the legal mind-set *that assumes life is supposed to be orderly, consistent, predictable, and regulable.*

This is one of the Law's great ironies. It wants so much to be objective. But its abstractions are saturated with implicit moralisms about how life should be. It expects too much, and when these expectations are not met—when life doesn't abide by the Law's idealized conventions—the Law compounds the problem by becoming more insistent, asserting more control, making a greater show of strength, and clamping down more firmly. But the harder the Law presses its abstract demands, the more irrepressible life seems, and the more frantic the Law becomes.

To re-establish contact with the ground of actual experience, lawyers must break through the abstractions that separate them from life below the clouds. They must come back to earth, where the air is thicker and more life-sustaining. In my experience, this means that lawyers need to educate their passions and invigorate their imaginations with the same dedication that they apply to sharpening their analytic skills. They must stop over-using mental habits like objectivity and adversity and become more adept at applying such specialized tools *only* when a particular job requires it. After all, few artists choose to use only two colors. Lawyers must learn to complement their professional mind-set with other perspectives, and find more appropriate ways of responding to the myriad opportunities and challenges of daily life.

All of us, for example, spend too much time trying to figure things out in advance. This isn't a problem until we make the next step of *insisting* that reality matches our plans. Take, for example, a company ablaze with the "lean and mean" managerial fad. A team of business planners makes economic projections for the company based on certain assumptions. One year later, the company hasn't met the desired goals. What to do? Question the efficacy of the projections themselves? Hell no. The answer of the planners is to fire more people in a short-term attempt to meet *what from the beginning were abstract goals.* It's as if the projections are trying to protect themselves by refusing to admit their own limitations. I am reminded of my days as a shoe salesman when grimacing customers would try to force their feet into shoes two sizes too small. "But I've *always* worn this size," they would say.

Another example of how we can let our abstractions rule us comes from therapy. A common lament, and one I hear from many lawyers, is "Who am I? I don't know who I am." The striking thing about this question is its implicit assumption that it can be "answered" at all. But how might we answer such a question? I don't mean what *is* the answer, but what form might such an answer take? Is it like the old joke that the answer to life is "43"? Can personal identity be so formulated? From a psychological point of view, "Who am I?" is but the tip of an ideological iceberg, the bulk of its supporting assumptions invisible to the eye of surface understanding.

Even as we are tormented by questions like "Who am I?" these very questions can tell us much about who we are at any given time. Think how differently such questions sound at sweet sixteen, or after losing our job at thirty, or when forced into retirement at sixty-five. Often, "Who am I?" identifies a person who believes that life and identity can be settled, given like a solution. There is potential danger here, because such a person might decide that if the question can't be answered then the answer must be, "I am nothing," or "Life is meaningless." One recalls the confused arrogance of the existentialists who tried to impose their personal sense of desperation on the world around them. Such people might appear to live apart from life, watching it from the vantage point of their abstractions. Such people might secretly feel out of control despite outward showings of order and competence, perhaps feeling as if their lives move only when sucked forward by the expectations of others. They might confuse looking at a map with going on vacation. And yet, for such a person, the mysterious "I" in "Who am I?" is nowhere more in evidence than in the sense of dislocation and intellectual estrangement found in the question itself.

III

In law school, lawyers are taught to analyze a case by finding out the facts, looking up the law, and then applying the law to the facts. This intellectual routine obviously has practical utility, but it breaks down when lawyers begin to apply it by rote. Then they have elevated an abstract method to cosmological status. But the soul is under no obligation to obey the Law's abstract mandates, and life is more than a series of examples gathered together to prove or disprove some theory.

We know that the sustaining and unifying themes of any discipline will necessarily contribute to that discipline's psychology. Therefore, the more a person couches his or her individuality in terms of professional identity, the more that person's psychological life will be influenced by the profession's most deeply held mental habits. *Ideas have psychological implications.* The stronger the ideas, or the more fiercely we embrace them, the deeper their psychological ramifications.

This ideational component of psychological life is especially influential among lawyers because of their highly trained intellectual capabilities and the strictness of the legal mind-set. We have seen how the Law attempts to force a legalistic overlay on everyday experience. We know, too, that the legal mind seeks to glean order out of chaos by imposing pre-formed philosophical constructs. The problem is that the Law's philosophical stance, not to mention its lock-step application, leaves too much out. It tends to empty ordinary experience of its passionate, emotional, and imaginative aspects—all of which are seen by the Law as interfering with its own definitions of stability, consistency, and predictability. At the same time, the Law becomes more anxious in the face of life's constant commotion and change, like a prim headmaster with a class of third graders.

The life of the soul, like the lives of us all, cannot be controlled in any but the basest manner by external regulation. Lawyers know this as well as anybody, but the constrictions of the legal mind-set suppress this instinctive knowledge. Like everybody else, lawyers want and need a fuller life, a life free from reductive and confining expectations, a life off the record. They know that a contented soul must live in accord with its intrinsic nature and temperament. But here the Law speaks up, warning lawyers not to open the floodgates of individuality, and demanding that they stay within the lines of the Law's defining abstractions. It isn't easy being a lawyer.

There is much in the life of the soul that seems paradoxical to the Law. But to be fair we must ask whether these paradoxes are intrinsic to psychological life or are imposed by a legalistic philosophy uncomfortable with apparent contradiction. Yes, lawyers must avoid investing their individuality solely in their professions, while at the same time becoming more intimately connected to their profession by respecting Law as a necessary work of and for soul. The legal mind needs deflation and inflation at once, both a revitalized regard for the everyday and a reaffirmation of the Law's inspirational well-springs. Lawyers must take it easier on themselves while also realizing that what they do has ultimate consequence. Such a life is a work in progress—as soon as we say one thing we have to say another, forever revising, editing, discovering, creating, forgetting. This is the kind of life that I believe the Law and lawyers hunger for, a life lived not as an observer but as a participant.

This isn't magic we're talking about here. If we limit ourselves to detached abstraction as a way of life, we will become cold. If we go through life assuming that everyone is trying to pull something on us, we will become lonely, paranoid, and anxious. If we insist that life obey predetermined rules, we will become frustrated and compulsive. If we look for argument in every discussion, we will become brutish and ignorant, obstacles to the very peace we proclaim as our mission. If we see ourselves as fungible fiduciaries or amoral technocrats in service to the bottom line, we will have problems with values. And if we see ourselves as aristocratic heroes holding back anarchy's common hordes, we will become condescending elitists, forlornly watching life in the courtyard from the killing protection of our high-rise towers.

CONTROLLING LAW

"So explain to me how you approach a legal dispute."

"The first thing you have to know are the basic facts so you can figure out in general what kind of legal issues might be involved, what kind of case it is. And then you need to know what the desired outcome is, what the client wants." The Law speaks carefully, as if giving a recipe. "As soon as possible, you want to determine what the controlling law is, and then really get a good hold on the facts."

"Controlling law?"

"Yes. You need to know what the general legal principles involved are, and then you need to gather case law to support your position. You have to read other cases like yours, especially cases from the relevant jurisdiction. The more analogous cases you can find that go your way, the better."

"What about cases going the other way? Cases that disagree with your position?"

"You have to prepare a defense to them, of course. Perhaps you can show they're legally irrelevant, or factually distinguishable, or something like that. There are always lots of defenses. Anyway, you continue to research the law and gather the facts more or less in tandem. Usually your legal research will require more refined factual investigation, and newly discovered facts often open up new legal issues. The theoretical legal goal, you might say, is to apply the controlling law to the facts of your case in a manner showing that the controlling law supports your position."

"So you find the relevant law, apply it to the facts of your case, and then argue that—based on the law and the facts—things should turn out your way?"

"That is grossly oversimplified, but yes, that's about it."

Note the Law's special focus on applying law to facts. But the Law also makes a more subtle point. Facts can "open up new legal issues." Instead of looking at facts primarily as passive receptors of legal analysis, this comment by the Law also suggests that facts can be considered as a generative ground for legal principles. Instead of only applying law to facts, we can also turn to facts for legal guidance.

This is hardly a new idea. Although we have been concentrating on the Law's tendency to rely on pre-formed abstractions, case law is the actual life-blood of the western legal tradition. Looked at from the ground up, it is the timeless deposit of cases that forms the basis for the Law's abstractions. The problems arise when the Law leaves this ground of support and begins to operate on the basis of abstract principles without reference to the facts of the case. When the Law loses touch with the facts, it begins to fly blind. By ignoring necessary details, the Law ensures that its abstract principles are never adequate to the precise realities of any particular case. Very often, in fact, the degree to which legal solutions fail to satisfy the complexities of a given case is a fair measure of how far away from the facts the Law has strayed, how far out it has become, and how badly it has overused its abstract capabilities to the detriment of fact-based wisdom.

Many people talk about the life of the Law and about how the Law is always changing and evolving. But left unspoken is the fact that the Law also is always dying, some parts of it already dead. That is what fact-based case law teaches us. The Law's abstract tendencies have trouble here, unable to accept the reality and inevitability of death, unable to let go, to close the cover on dead letter law. Think how many outdated laws are still on the books and how many tired prejudices still linger in the halls of justice.

Increasingly we feel that the laws by which our lives are regulated are out of touch with our actual needs. We imagine our politicians as insiders who craft laws for elite groups of privileged self-interest, all the while denying our own complicity in giving these insiders their necessary grass-roots support, as if nobody voted for them. (Some compound this denial by calling for *more laws* to protect us from our own apathy. "Please," they say, "stop me from voting for an incumbent.") We talk freely about special interest groups buying votes, but less so about our willingness to sell. As a result of all this, the Law seems increasingly arbitrary and patch-worked. We begin to sense that the Law is playing by rules foreign to our native sensibilities. The Law becomes oppressive, monolithic, irrefutable. Meanwhile, we grow more and more anxious when the Law is around because we know the danger of a tightly wound spring. We know that the same Law that praises predictability can also be capricious, sometimes even vengeful and mean.

Here again is that lingering sense of dissociation with which we began this last chapter. It isn't only the Law or lawyers who are lonely. The world that they draw away from also feels the loss. Think how often we feel abandoned by the Law, how often disappointed, and how often forsaken in our faith. Think how, when we bemoan the lack of law and order, we also are expressing grief and anger at the Law for letting us down and leaving us behind on our own. There's never a cop when you need one, we say.

One way through this impasse is to increase our appreciation for the facts of our communal existence. In particular, the Law must learn to give more attention and respect to facts, because *facts are the Law's only visceral connection to soul*. The facts of the case must be the Law's guide, and the Law must learn to resist the temptation of its training by refusing to manipulate facts to achieve this or that adversarial advantage. The Law is already good, maybe too good, at inventing defensible theories. *It needs to become better at making imaginative connections with a given set of facts and then crafting suitable legal responses based on those facts.* In other words, the Law needs to make more art and fewer knock-offs.

III

It isn't up to psychology, any more than to economics, to provide the Law and lawyers with constitutive images. We cannot care for the soul of the Law from the outside through transient ideologies or managerial fads. If renewed imagination is called for, it must emerge from lawyers' dedication to recovering the soulful dimensions of their own work.

The way to soul is through a radical appreciation of the

imaginative dimensions of legal practice. The sources for this imaginal revolution are already there in daily practice: in messy cases that refuse categorization, in the mysterious search for motives, the cathedraled architecture of the courthouse, the dance of negotiation, and the lawyer's carefully reasoned fictions. But we have to pay close attention or we'll miss the soul's many quiet voices. We must turn down our volume and lean in close to listen, straining to catch every nuance, every sentiment. To paraphrase a beautiful old legal phrase, *anima ipsa loquitur*—the soul speaks for itself.

ENDNOTES

1.   L. Eron and R. Redmount. The Effect of Legal Education on Attitudes. *Journal of Legal Education* 9 (1957): 441. Cited in G. Benjamin, A. Kaszniak, B. Sales, and S. Shanfield. The Role of Legal Education in Producing Psychological Distress among Law Students and Lawyers. *American Bar Foundation Research Journal* 2 (1986): 251.

2.   R. Kugelmann. 1982. Hammering Metaphor from Metal: A Psychology of Stress. *Spring: An Annual of Archetypal Psychology and Jungian Thought,* p. 254.

3.   *Ibid.,* p. 253.

4.   S. Keen. 1991. *Fire in the Belly.* New York: Bantam, p. 61.

5.   "Objects could now properly be 'held' rather than possessed. . . . Thousands of topographical descriptions have come down to us from this period; *boundaries became effective* through these descriptions. . . . *This appropriative description of reality began as a jurisprudential method before it became the foundation of natural sciences.*" (Italics mine.) I. Illich and B. Sanders. 1988. *The Alphabetization of the American Mind.* San Francisco: North Point Press, pp. 35–36.

6.   See note on sundials and oriental timekeeping in: J. Hillman. 1979. *The Dream and the Underworld.* New York: Harper & Row, pp. 224–25 n.10.

7.   R. B. Onians. 1951. *The Origins of European Thought.* Cambridge: Cambridge University Press, pp. 411–15.

8.   Hillman, *Dream and the Underworld,* pp. 224–25 n.10.

9.   W. Eaton, J. Anthony, W. Mandel, and R. Garrison. Occupations and the Prevalence of Major Depressive Disorder. *Journal of Occupational Medicine* 32, no. 11 (1990): 1083–85.

10.   G. Benjamin, E. Darling, and B. Sales. The Prevalence of Depression, Alcohol Abuse, and Cocaine Abuse among United States Lawyers. *International Journal of Law and Psychiatry* 13, no. 3 (1990): 241.

11.   Eaton, Major Depressive Disorder, pp. 1083–85.

12.   Washington State Bar Association Lawyers' Assistance Program Staff. February 1988. Are Lawyers Distressed . . . And How?! *Washington State Bar News,* p. 13.

13.   American Bar Association. 1991. *The State of the Legal Profession,* p. 17.

14.   Commission on Women in the Profession. 1990. Lawyers and Balanced Lives: A Guide to Drafting and Implementing Workplace Policies for Lawyers. American Bar Association, introduction at p. 5.

15.   American Bar Association, *State of the Profession,* p. 20. The exact numbers were sixty percent of male lawyers and fifty-four percent of female lawyers. Similarly, law students in one study stated that there was no professor in the law school who was taking a special interest in their academic progress (eighty-four percent), or to whom they could turn for personal advice (seventy-one percent). C. Auerbach. Legal Education and Some of its Discontents. *Journal of Legal Education* 34 (1984): 57. Cited in Benjamin, Psychological Distress among Law Students and Lawyers, p. 249.

16.   American Bar Association, *State of the Profession,* p. 52. The Maryland Bar Association's Special Committee on Law Practice Quality found that one-third of the lawyers they surveyed were dissatisfied with their practice. A survey of one thousand lawyers by the National Law Journal revealed that only thirty-one percent of the respondents were very satisfied with their careers. M. Fisk. May 28, 1990. A Measure of Satisfaction: What America's Lawyers Think about the Profession and Their Peers. *The National Law Journal,* supp. at p. 2.

17. P. Blachly, H. Osterud, and R. Josslin. 1963. Suicide in Professional Groups. *New England Journal of Medicine* 268, no. 23 (1963): 1280. A report discussing surveys of Washington and Arizona lawyers noted that of the high percentage of lawyers suffering from depression, "most were experiencing suicidal ideation. In addition, they typically isolated themselves . . . which greatly exacerbates the risk of their acting upon suicidal ideation." The authors concluded that lawyers "are at a much greater risk of not only acting upon their suicidal ideation but of also being lethal during an attempt." Benjamin, Prevalence of Depression, p. 241.

18. ABA Center for Professional Responsibility. 1991. p. 10. *Interim Report of the Committee on Civility of the Seventh Federal Judicial Circuit,* p. 10.

19. A poll in Texas showed that substance abuse accounted for approximately fifteen to twenty percent of all grievance complaints filed against lawyers. Sales. 1989. The Lawyer's Assistance Program: A Responsible and Effective Alternative for the Substance-Impaired Lawyer. *Texas Bar Journal* 52:273. In Georgia, substance abuse is implicated in fifty to seventy-five percent of all disciplinary cases, approximately sixty-five percent of all lawyer malpractice cases, and over eighty percent of disciplinary cases involving the misuse of client funds. Elliott. 1989. Lawyers Helping Lawyers. *Georgia State Bar Journal* 25:113. A study by the Oregon State Bar Professional Liability Fund found that out of a hundred randomly selected legal malpractice suits, sixty percent were filed against lawyers suffering from substance abuse. Cited in Benjamin, Prevalence of Depression, p. 244. An ABA commission concluded that "Other bars have estimated that forty to seventy-five percent of all [disciplinary] complaints stem from lawyer impairment."

20. D. Spillis. 1990. Lawyer Substance Abuse. *Issues Update 1990.* American Bar Association, p. 7.

21. Benjamin, Prevalence of Depression, p. 244.

22. A. Elwork and G. Benjamin. 1993. Lawyers in Distress. Unpublished manuscript, pp. 13–14.

23. Eaton, Major Depressive Disorder, pp. 1084–85.

24. Benjamin, Prevalence of Depression, p. 241.

25. For an extended discussion of religion and suicide, see: J. Hillman. 1976. *Suicide and the Soul*. Dallas: Spring Publications.

26. J. Hillman. 1983. *Inter Views*. New York: Harper & Row, p. 172.

27. A. Chroust. The Legal Profession in Ancient Athens. *Notre Dame Lawyer* 29 (1954): 339.

28. M. Watkins. 1987. "In Dreams Begin Responsibilities": Moral Imagination and Peace. In *Facing Apocalypse*, eds. V. Andrews, R. Bosnak, and K. Goodwin, pp. 73–76. Dallas: Spring Publications.

29. *The Random House Dictionary of the English Language*. 1987. New York: Random House.

30. H. Berman. The Background of the Western Legal Tradition in the Folklaw of the Peoples of Europe. *University of Chicago Law Review* 45 (1978): 553.